THE SACRAMENTS

THE
SACRAMENTS

DISCOVERING THE TREASURES OF DIVINE LIFE

FR. MATTHEW KAUTH

SAINT BENEDICT✛PRESS

Charlotte, North Carolina

Nihil Obstat: Reverend Jason Christian, STL
               Censor Deputatus

Imprimatur: Most Reverend Peter J. Jugis, JCD
               Bishop of Charlotte
               June 29, 2018
               Solemnity of Sts. Peter and Paul

The nihil obstat and imprimatur are official declarations that a book is free from doctrinal or moral error. No implication is contained therein that those who grant the nihil obstat or imprimatur agree with the contents, opinions, or statements expressed.

Cover design by Caroline K. Green

ISBN: 978-1-5051-1142-2

Published in the United States by
Saint Benedict Press
PO Box 410487
Charlotte, NC 28241
www.SaintBenedictPress.com

Printed in the United States of America

Contents

PREFACE

You have just done a courageous and dangerous thing. You have opened a book. You have given an unknown author a moment of your time. Your eyes are seeing words and your mind is quickly reducing those words into ideas. Each word you read, by definition, alters you. It is courageous.

Given the nature of this book, it is dangerous as well, but only dangerous to an old life you no longer want. We tend to think of our physical, concrete life as the only real life. Yet is it not true that the interior life is the one that alone has "meaning" for us?

What do we find in our interior? We want more life, maybe even a different life. How often it is that we want to make a new start? We change a look, an address, or even friends, hoping that we will not drag the life we lived before along with us. We want to turn to something new in the hope that it will be different and provide for us what we have lacked up to that point. That desire is quite reasonable. Natural desires have natural objects to which they correspond. If I have hunger, it's a pretty good indication that there must be an object of that desire, namely food. It doesn't mean, as C. S. Lewis once quipped, that we will be able to obtain the food, but it does mean that we are the kinds of beings who replicate our cells by eating.

All of our natural desires have objects which are relatively within our grasp. Yet, when all those objects are obtained, we hear those words once spoken to the rich man by Jesus Christ: "One thing you still lack" (Lk 18:22). What is that one thing? You lack the fullness of eternal life, which Christ defines for us in the Scriptures: "And this is eternal life, that they know you the only true God, and Jesus Christ whom you have sent" (Jn 17:3). This knowledge is more than hearing or reading words. This knowledge is a participation in the life of the Word himself. St. Peter writes in his second letter: "His divine power has granted to us all things that pertain to life and godliness, through the knowledge of him who called us to his own glory and excellence, by which he has granted to us his precious and very great promises, that through these you may escape from the corruption that is in the world because of passion, and become partakers of the divine nature" (1:3–5). We escape one life—that is, the life of futile corruption which we have all experienced—and enter into the divine life by actually participating in a divine nature.

My interior life was made to be a place that is inhabited. We have all experienced the enthusiasm of infatuation when the gravitational force of love draws us, almost unwillingly, toward another. Our interior life becomes consumed with the other. The new beloved takes up so much mental space! We think about them in all things and love the thoughts we think. We interiorly orbit the beloved who dwells inside of us in a kind of mental existence. But because the hold is tenuous, we need the other to renew their sentiments with great frequency. When the object of our love is only another transitory human being, it makes for a volatile interior life. It is hardly a position of stability to cling tightly to another who is himself or herself also falling. Yet, when one is known to be loved and loves in return, there is a certain interior fullness.

What infatuation shows is that we were not made to be alone in the interior life. We are dwelling places. The very nature of motherhood is one incarnate sign that persons are made to dwell in persons. We are made in the image of a Triune God who is himself three Persons in one nature. We resemble this as his image. We long to live in others and have others live in us. It is not sufficient to simply dwell bodily with others. A herd on the hillside does as much. We want to know and be known, to love and to be loved. We desire to have someone who dwells in our interior life.

There is a curious passage in St. Matthew's Gospel that talks about interior indwelling: "When the unclean spirit has gone out of a man, he passes through waterless places seeking rest, but he finds none. Then he says, 'I will return to my house from which I came.' And when he comes he finds it empty, swept, and put in order. Then he goes and brings with him seven other spirits more evil than himself, and they enter and dwell there; and the last state of that man becomes worse than the first" (Mt 12:43–45). The house of a man's soul might be swept and put in order, but if it remains uninhabited, it becomes a haunted house. We are made to be dwelling places, *but for whom*?

When we enter into friendship with others, there is a true consolation (which means to be with us in our solitude). As much of a consolation as it might be, we quickly find that it is not yet sufficient. There is one thing we still lack. Just as we were not made merely for a human life, we were also not made to be the dwelling place simply of other humans. We were made to be the dwelling place of God. We were meant to participate in divine life. But what does this mean exactly?

Imagine, if you will, the possibility of dwelling in another perfectly, rather than by virtue of that person thinking about you and being of the same mind and heart. What if one could dwell in someone else and actually use their mind and heart as their own? St. Paul says that we have the mind of Christ (1 Cor 2:16). Further, God's love is said to be poured into our hearts by the Holy Spirit (Rom 5:5). Is this to say that I can have his thoughts? That I can have his love, as if these were my own to use? What sort of a communion is this? This is persons dwelling most intimately in persons! "It is no longer I who live but Christ who lives in me (Gal. 2:20)."

This is exactly what the sacraments effect, and this book is offered as an attempt to assist you to have this life, and to have it abundantly.

INTRODUCTION

How did you come by this book? Was it given by your pastor at a Christmas or Easter Mass? Was it passed on by a friend or meddling in-law? Did you make your way into a darkened church hoping to light a candle, to enkindle some hope, to find some meaning, to beg for mercy, and there the book was lying on the pew? One thing is certain: as I sit and write these words, I have no idea where they will go. And yet there is One who does.

Who is that One? He is God. Can God tell the future? As I sit and write, how does he know where and when these words will be read? The answer is simpler than you might at first think. Perhaps an example will help.

Let us agree for the sake of argument that, when you finish reading this sentence, you will close the book momentarily and stand up; after standing up, you will sit down again and continue reading. (Ready? Go!)

Did you do it? Did I foretell the future? Certainly not. You could have simply kept reading. Most of you likely did. However, if you did decide to follow the instructions, you could have paused at the word *go* and predicted the future. Had you done so, it would have gone something like this: "I predict that I will close this book, stand up, sit back down, open the book again, and continue reading." Once you had done so, you could have truly claimed that you predicted the future.

How did you know? You knew because the action was in your power. You *caused* it. It is true that, at the very moment you were about to do it, a bird could have flown at you and startled you, your friend could have returned and asked you to leave, or any number of things *could* have intervened to prevent you from fulfilling the future you predicted. Nevertheless, you had a pretty good chance—it was relatively within your power—to cause the future.

We speak about God as being all-powerful because reason demands that he be so if he were God. Along with reason, revelation tells us that he is indeed all-powerful. If he is omnipotent, if nothing that is possible lies outside the realm of his causal power, nothing can therefore "stop" him from causing. If we use the example above, there could be no intervening action that would or could impede his "prediction" (literally meaning to speak before something) of events. He must cause, on some level, all things that exist.

It is thus that he perfectly sees the future. What is the future? It doesn't exist. Does God see all things as simultaneous or simultaneously see all things? He necessarily sees all things that exist since he is the cause. Now here we run into a bit of a problem between God's causal activity and that of our own activity. Did you choose to close the book and stand up? If you did, did God do it or did you? This is one of those deep philosophical problems that lie outside the scope of this practical book, but the initial part of an answer is necessary for our purposes.

This is a fact: you never act alone. Everything you do is

predicated on his causal activity. In other words, for you to be and thus to do things (take actions) necessitates his prior and sustaining activity. This does not mean that you do not have certain causal power. On the contrary, he offers us the greatest causal power of any creatures we encounter. In short, every act we engage in is undergirded with an act of God. We always act together, and even if sometimes our actions are deficient, his are not.

Why would I get us stuck in the thickets of bewildering philosophical questions? Because what this truth reveals is both frightening and comforting. I mentioned previously that you were made to be a dwelling place for another. I noted that persons dwell in persons. In some sense, you can never get away from him. He is always present to you by his causal power. St. Augustine once said that God is higher than the highest in me and more intimate to me than my inner most self.[1]

This means he has always known that you would be reading this. He has always known that I would be writing this. His knowledge did not simply cause it to happen or "make it happen." Nevertheless, he knows it since his causal power is necessary for it to occur. He does not know it in the same fashion as you and I might know the score of the Packers vs. the Panthers game, a simple data point that has little to no importance to my life (unless, of course, I am a Cheesehead). He knows it as a matter of Providence. That word means to "see ahead" and, thus, to "provide" for. His Wisdom "orders all things sweetly" to the end of his loving purpose (Ws 8:1). To put it more poetically and simply, this means that he never takes his eyes off you. It means that you are an object of his

---

[1]   *Interior intimo meo et superior summo meo.* Confessions III, 6, 11.

love and a subject of his thought. It means that such is his love that were you the only creature he had ever created, he would have nevertheless died to redeem you. It means that you are known and you are wanted. It also means, incidentally, that it might not just be an "accident" that this book fell into your hands, nor that I am writing it. God is not proud and uses whatever instruments are in his good pleasure to bring about an end far beyond our own activity, the end of you and I sharing in his Divine life. My writing and you reading can be causes of you and I growing in divine life as we are both now acting as instruments in a loose sense of God's activity.

In short, while I do choose things and cause things, there is One whose choosing is supreme and whose causing is in all things. Have you ever noticed how you thought you were choosing something randomly only to find that it wasn't random at all? He brought a thousand things to bear on that moment that could have only happened by a coordination of a thousand threads of human volition to make you arrive at the present tapestry. It is wondrous when you begin to notice these "signs" of his movements.

That is why opening this book and reading it is courageous. It is in some sense a response to him. To stop and take a look at him. To give him your attention. The book and certainly the author are of no real importance except insofar as they assist in facilitating that encounter.

Stop and consider God and his actions in history, the history of his saving grace and his actions in your life. The word "to consider" ironically comes from two Latin words: *cum* + *sidera* which means "with the stars." In other words, we do not have much light by which to see (starlight); yet the stars, as the philosophers once said, are those first things which cause us to wonder. Taking time to examine things, even those things difficult to see, evokes in us desire (*de* + *sidera,* or "from the stars"). If that which we behold is good, it generates a desire to attain that good. But what if the good we see is too much for us?

When the people witnessed Jesus of Nazareth teaching and healing, they were struck with wonder, which is a kind of fear. This fear arises from the mind's inability to understand what it sees. It is not the kind of fear that makes you want to run away and hide necessarily, but it could. It is the sort of fear that comes from seeing something so great that you feel yourself in danger. Thus, if you begin to look and looking makes you wonder because you behold something so great, you will also grow in fear. Let me give you an example.

The summer before entering into college, some friends and I decided to drive across the country, the usual rite of passage for a young man. In the middle of the night, when my companions were fast asleep, I saw a sign for Mt. Rushmore. Having never seen it, I didn't want to miss the opportunity. Despite it being dark, I had assumed it would be well lit and I could do a drive-by.

I pulled off the highway and followed the serpentine road to the parking lot. Before climbing out of the car, I left my sleeping friends with a quick note—"Mt. Rushmore – come see if you like"—and began to walk along the paved parkway. To my surprise, the park was not locked (this was many years ago). I was walking for some time along an unlit path when I heard the low rumble of an impending storm. Nothing but increased darkness greeted me as I waltzed along until suddenly my stomach was struck by a metal bar. So thick was the night that I had walked right into a guardrail. I grabbed the rail by both hands and was just about to hop over it when a bolt of lightning shot through the canvas of clouds, illuminating in a most horrific fashion two dreadful realities: 1) four massive stone faces and 2) a deep canyon separating me from the faces, just on the other side of that bar I was about to illegally hurdle.

The result? Fear. I was ushered in front of two realities which, when lit by the dazzling and immediate fire of lightning, proved no match for my youthful fearlessness. Most likely I screamed. I cannot recall. What I do recall is that I sat there immobile, my eyes toggling back and forth from the now slightly illumined faces (dawn was approaching and their outlines were vaguely visible) to the valley below. With the former, I had grown accustomed. It ceased to be a cause of fear. Those faces were simply the four presidents carved in stone. The latter gained my respect as something that had nearly welcomed me to her depths as the last jump of my life. The effect of the whole was a sense of awe. Two things which were larger than my bodily life confronted me. It was at first dreadful but it burned into my memory an analogy which has proved useful.

We are not trying to look at Mt. Rushmore. We are trying to look at God and his activity in Christ and in the sacraments. What do we see when we begin to look at God? God is not small. He is not large. He is great. He is awesome in the truest sense. To begin to walk toward him is a walk in darkness. He is not an object of our senses, having no body. He is infinite and I am finite. He is all-powerful and I am weak. He is truth and I am deceitful. He is goodness and I am sinful. He is beauty and in my unloveliness, I hide. Unlike Mt. Rushmore, I don't grow accustomed to his Presence as the light grows. On the contrary, in some sense I become more fearful, but it is a fear of the Lord and the first stage of Wisdom. It is the beginning because that fear is the effect of first beginning to see. To see what? In the words of God the Father to St. Catherine, God is "He who is" and I am "he who is not."

Yet that is only half of the truth. I was made to live with him. I was created to enjoy his love and to be an object of his delight. Is it true that he so loved the world that he sent his only beloved Son that I might have life and have a share in his life? All this is true. It is written on every page of Scripture and every page of your history.

How do I possibly live with such a God? I am mortal. I experience suffering and I inflict it. I experience evil and I commit it. I do not do the good I want but rather I often do the evil I do not want (Rom 7:19). I have human desires that have human ends, so how can I be expected to live like the angels? If I had been there at the Sea of Galilee, maybe it would have been different. If I had heard his voice and witnessed his miracles, perhaps I, too, would have left everything and followed him. But where is he now? What is he doing? We are left with a memory of his action, a promise of a heavenly future, and a present too often filled with sadness and anxiety.

May I attempt an answer? You have been courageous thus far. *Noli timere!* Do not be afraid! The only thing that is ultimately in danger should you read further is the life of the "old man." The only thing God will not let live forever if you are to live with him is a life that is not in him. C. S. Lewis once remarked that God may love you despite your sinfulness, but never because of it. As One who loves you infinitely, he cannot and will not stop without an ultimate refusal to attempt to destroy the reign of sin in us. He cannot cease to attempt to unbind, to set us free to live in the truth of the sons and daughters of God.

What follows is a description of his activity. What is he doing now? He gives life, he strengthens, he nourishes, he heals, and he makes us coworkers with him in the building up of his Body, the Church. We call his activity sacraments. Have you received his activity? If you have, why hasn't it changed you? Do you live a divine life or merely a human life? How do I live a sacramental life and, thus, live a divine life?

It is the purpose of this book to answer these questions. But first, we must understand what sacraments are and why, in his Divine Wisdom, Christ has ordered his activity in and through them.

CHAPTER 1

WHAT IS A SACRAMENT?[2]

THE WORD BECAME FLESH AND DWELT AMONG US

Nestled on a rocky perch overlooking the Adriatic is a town called Loreto. Catholics fortunate enough to have had some training in the recitation of the Holy Rosary may be familiar with the "Litany of Loreto." These august titles of the Mother of God swirled historically around a small house found at the center of this town, encased in marble and further enclosed in a massive basilica. It is the house of the Mother of God from Nazareth.

This house was brought to Loreto in the thirteenth century (by the angels, as tradition has it) and is rightly an

---

[2] The word *sacramentum* has an etymologically rich history. It has been used to speak about sacred things (sacra), mysteries, oaths, and signs. While all of these play a roll in what we know as the seven sacraments, I will be focusing on sacrament as a sign. The classic definition of a sacrament is useful: a sacrament is an outward sign instituted by Christ to give grace (Cf. *Summa Theologiae*, III, q. 60 a. 1).

epicenter of Marian pilgrimages. The first time I went there as a young priest, I found out why. I went into this home of the Virgin Mother, knelt down, and began to pray. As I looked up toward the altar, I caught sight of a familiar Latin phrase from the Gospel of John. Inscribed in marble at the base of the altar were the words *Et Verbum caro factum est,* "And the Word became flesh" (Jn 1:14). What I was not expecting to see was one small word attached to this oft-quoted phrase. That word was *hic,* "here." The Word of God became flesh *here.*

I was immediately confronted with events that were not mythical, events that were not imaginary. Here. Not nowhere. Here. An angel of God was sent to the town of Nazareth to a Virgin betrothed to a man named Joseph *here.* The Virgin's name was Mary and she lived *here.* She touched *these* stones. These stones witnessed the Incarnation of the Son of God in her womb with the utterance of her *fiat:* "Let it be done to me according to your word" (Lk 1:38).

I remained wrapped in silent wonder, but the very stones began to cry out in my interior (Lk 19:40): "We were there! It happened in our midst and in our walls. We covered this mystery silent as stone and protected it. We stones witnessed the divine babe return from Egypt. We sheltered him from wind and rain. Here he played. Here he laughed. Here he loved." And I was inside these stone walls, allowed into the home where my true Home was. In a certain place, at a certain time, in a certain woman, God became man. He was *located* and could be visited, seen, touched, and heard. Loreto does not allow the reality and particularity of God's incarnation to turn into misty myth. It is flesh and bone. It is real and hard as stone. It happened. But why did it happen?

WHY DID GOD BECOME MAN?

Previously we asked the question: "How am I to live with such a God?" In the beginning, as the book of Genesis tells us, we lived in intimacy with God without fear or shame. While that intimacy was not yet the fullness of Divine indwelling, we did dwell in communion with him. The temptation in the Garden could only be directed to that thing which "we still lacked." We were tempted to have the fullness of life without Life himself. We were tempted and attempted to become like God without God.

This is what tradition calls original sin. Its effect—the loss of Divine friendship—is our inheritance. The maddening irony is that we *were* created to be "like God." This gift of participation in his life, by which we become more and more like him, is called grace. It makes us pleasing to him and makes us his sons and daughters. This grace of justification and sonship was lost, and the bitter tale of history, the vanity of vanities, became our lot.

Yet, in a deeper wisdom and perfect act of divine irony, God became man and offered his life in perfect obedience, even unto death on the cross. This act of Redemption is now the means through which you and I can have access to God and truly become sons and daughters in the Son. In other words, we desired to become like God, now God has become like man, but man obedient unto death, man crucified and risen. We wanted to become like God, and now we receive what we wanted. We must become like God—but now the Godman crucified in order to become like the Godman risen.

The means by which this is accomplished in us are the sacraments. As the old adage goes, God became man so that man in turn might become like God. This sublime possibility was not relegated to first-century Palestine. As Adam was the "head" of all men in creation, Christ is the Head of all men in the new Creation. To be part of his Body is to be a member (like my hand is a bodily member) of his Mystical Body, the Church. This does not mean that others live with the memory of his actions and imitate him. While well-intentioned, such banalities as "what would Jesus do" leave us in a sphere of activity that is merely human. What *is* he doing now?[3] The Head and Body act together as one. *Redemptor mundi, salva nos!* Redeemer of the world, save us! He is at work saving us. He does this by incorporating us into his life (literally making us into the Body). He acts now in the world, employing instruments both living and non-living to bring all things into one in him (Eph 1:10).

HOW DID HE REDEEM US?

Christ assumed to himself a human nature in the bridal chamber of Our Lady's womb. It was there, as we noted, that he forever united to himself in a perfect union the two natures of God and man in his Person as Son. Christ is God and man, one Person with two distinct but not divided natures. For our purposes, a nature is what you are born with, that principle

---

3   See, for example, the passage of John 5:16–17: "And this was why the Jews persecuted Jesus, because he did this on the Sabbath. But Jesus answered them, 'My Father is working still, and I am working.'" "Christ now at the right hand of the Father lives to make intercession for us. He is at work. Consequently he is able for all time to save those who draw near to God through him, since he always lives to make intercession for them" (Heb 7:25).

of determination and power. What kind of nature does something have? We can answer that by watching what it can do.

Action follows upon being. Fish can swim, birds can fly, and humans can reason and love. It is a kind of power directed toward a certain end. Jesus Christ, having assumed a human nature to himself in the womb of the Blessed ever-Virgin Mary, has, therefore, two natures, divine and human. This means, of course, that he has the power to walk as a man and walk *on water* by the power of God. His human nature is like ours in all things but sin. His divine nature is omnipotent. These natures are neither confused nor separated but are perfectly united in the Second Person of the Blessed Trinity, the Son.

What does his human nature allow him to do which his divine nature alone "cannot" do? Recall the scene of the Wedding Feast at Cana. The Blessed Mother says to Jesus: "They have no wine" (Jn 2:3). No doubt she sees further than the simple lack of preparation. Is this the time of fulfillment? Is this the moment when the true Bridegroom will provide "pure choice wine" for his people in the wedding feast of God with his people (Is 25)?

In a terse yet powerful response, Christ asks his mother in turn: "O woman, what have you to do with me?" (Jn 2:4). His hour, the hour of his passion, the hour in which he would provide the true wine of his precious blood, had not yet come. Fr. John Banister Tabb poetically describes this scene, answering our question above. What does the human nature allow Christ to do? When his mother tells him they have no wine, he answers as follows (note the last line is spoken by the Blessed Mother):

> *What, woman, is my debt to thee,*
> *That I should not deny*

The boon thou dost demand of me?
'I gave thee power to die.'

Christ's human nature, assumed in the womb of the ever-Virgin Mother, gives him the power to die. Yet Christ does not merely have life, he *is* life. That life will confront death on the cross, conquer it, and rise to a new and everlasting life. The application of this life and our incorporation into Christ's new risen life will follow this pattern. The sacraments are incarnational (*in* + *carne,* "in the flesh").

INCARNATIONAL PRINCIPLE OF THE SACRAMENTS: WORD AND MATTER

What happened in that Holy House is analogous to what happens in the sacraments. The angel Gabriel spoke words to the Virgin. The Virgin received those words and commanded that it be done to her by God according to that word. And the Word himself became flesh.

What is a word? It is something sensible. I can hear it if spoken and see it if written. Yet it is more than matter. It carries with it something spiritual. It communicates an idea through the medium of matter. As St. Augustine once said, I can hear a word, but even when the sound is no more, the content of that word is not gone, it is in me. A word is an intelligible sign of something else, an idea, a concept that is communicated through the sign. In this sense, the Fathers said that Our Lady "conceived" through her ear. She heard the words and received them and conceived the Word himself.

In Sacred Scripture, God creates through his Word by speaking creation: *Let there be. . . .* His word is *causative.* He speaks and it comes to be. Isaiah the prophet eloquently articulates this point: "For as the rain and the snow come down from heaven, and do not return there but water the earth, making it bring forth and sprout, giving seed to the sower and bread to the eater, so shall my word be that goes forth from my mouth; it shall not return to me empty, but it shall accomplish that which I intend, and prosper in the thing for which I sent it" (Is 55:10–11).

In this image, the word of God returns to him. He speaks and that word returns, having fulfilled the purpose for which he spoke. This word is unlike our words. This word is his Wisdom. This Word is his Son. St. John thus writes, "In the beginning was the Word, and the Word was with God, and the Word was God" (Jn 1:1). This Word was spoken in time to the patriarchs and prophets. A prophet is someone who speaks another's word. This is indicated by the formula so often repeated by the prophets: "The word of the Lord came to me thus" and "thus says the Lord." The word of God is spoken by another. This can only ever be in varied, limited, and fragmentary ways (cf. Heb 1:1). When the Word assumes to himself a human nature, we have the fullness of Revelation. The Word of God will accomplish the purpose for which he was sent, namely, to reveal, to redeem, and to ultimately save.

Christ the Eternal Word uses words, and those words have power. The Roman Centurion knows this. When he asks Christ to heal his servant, he pleads for the Master not to come. Rather, "Only say the word, and my servant will be healed" (Mt 8:8). Christ is said to be one who speaks with authority, not like the scribes (see Mt 7:29). When asked why they did not capture Jesus, the soldiers reporting to the chief priests and Pharisees simply stated as their reason for failure: "No man ever spoke like this man" (Jn 7:46). The Apostles, too, know the power of his words, for even when all had left him on account of his teaching on the Holy Eucharist, they could not. When Jesus asks them: "'Will you also go away?' Simon Peter answered him, 'Lord, to whom shall we go? You have the words of eternal life; and we have believed, and have come to know, that you are the Holy One of God'" (Jn 6:67–69).

Even though Christ's words are efficacious (meaning they accomplish what they signify), *he nevertheless often employs matter in his actions.* Why does he make clay out of dirt and spittle, refashioning a blind man's eyes (Jn 9:6) when he could simply have spoken? Why does he put his fingers into a deaf man's ears? Why the spitting and touching the man's tongue while proclaiming, "Be opened!" (Mk 7:33–34)? Whether Christ speaks words or uses his hands to touch and heal, he employs his human nature as an instrument of his Divine nature. Before, we noted that his humanity gave him the power to die, but it also is the instrument through which he gives life, ultimately through his very death.

In summary, the Word became flesh, and that Word speaks through human words to reveal. He acts through a human body to heal. He dies in a human body to give life. Finally, in fulfillment of a passage from the prophet Jeremiah: "Your words were found and I ate them, and your words became to me a joy and the delight of my heart" (Jer 15:16). The Word made flesh would also give himself as food, to be not only heard, seen, and understood but devoured, consumed, and to become our joy and the delight of our hearts.

What Christ once did in the flesh, he now does in the sacraments.[4] The sacraments take their power from those very

---

4   Jesus's words and actions during his hidden life and public ministry

events in the life of Christ, principally from his passion. Just as water and blood flowed forth from the side of Christ (a sign not only of Baptism and the Holy Eucharist but of all the sacraments), so too do the sacraments now come forth from Christ in his Mystical Body, the Church. How does he do this? In a manner analogous to the Incarnation, Christ the Word acts. The Word brings forth his power by uniting his efficacious words with matter through a minister. We will explore this reality in each of the sacraments, but first we must understand what is meant by instrumentality.

INSTRUMENTALITY OF THE SACRAMENTS

We are all familiar with using instruments. The word in Greek is *organon*, which is where we get the word *organ* (whether those in your body or the one in your church which is played on Sunday). If I write a letter, I employ a pen. That pen has certain capacities which allow me to communicate my concepts through the mediums of ink and design to arrive at another creature who has the capacity to read them. Am I doing one thing and the pen doing another? On the contrary, it is one act of writing a letter. I, the principal agent, am the one who can give through that pen something spiritual,

---

were already salvific, for they anticipated the power of his Paschal mystery. They announced and prepared what he was going to give the Church when all was accomplished. The mysteries of Christ's life are the foundations of what he would henceforth dispense in the sacraments, through the ministers of his Church, for "what was visible in our Savior has passed over into his mysteries" (*Catechism of the Catholic Church*, no. 1115). Christ himself has instituted each of the seven sacraments (see ibid., no. 1114).

namely, the concepts being transmitted. It is more truly said that I write the letter and not the pen. Nevertheless, I do not write the letter without the pen. *We act in a unified manner.*

Christ used his humanity as his conjoined instrument, perfectly united to him, to affect our redemption in death. His Divinity is the principle agent of giving us Divine life. His human nature cannot give Divine life. Yet that Divine life is given to us through Christ's human nature as the Head of the Body, the Church. The sacraments are Christ's actions whereby he gives Divine grace through his humanity and employs further instruments as causes. For example, the pen is not part of my nature as my hand is. It can be said that I use my hand as an instrument which is part of my nature and the pen as that which I hold. The latter is less united than the former. So too the sacraments are "held" by Christ like a pen. He instrumentally employs water, oil, bread, et cetera. The Principle agent is Christ, and the secondary agents are elements of matter and the human ministers. They act, however, in a unified way to achieve something together infinitely beyond what the created elements alone could achieve.

There is, however, one more aspect that needs to be considered. Words. As I noted, the Incarnation was the Eternal Word taking flesh. So too the sacraments are a union of word and matter employed by Christ to bring about a determined end (new life, forgiveness of sins, union with his Body, et cetera). The power of the "spoken word" is seen in the act of creation, in the actions of Christ (he rebukes the storm in Lk 8:24) but also has its occasions in the Old Testament by the ministers of God.[5]

---

5   What is similar about magic and the sacraments? Magic was
     originally an attempt to manipulate and dominate matter. The

THE ROCK AND THE WORDS

There is a curious passage in the twentieth chapter of the book of Numbers. After Moses and Aaron had led the people of Israel from captivity through the desert to the promised land, they were not themselves permitted to enter. Why? Read the passage and see:

> Now there was no water for the congregation; and they assembled themselves together against Moses and against Aaron. And the people contended with Moses, and said, "Would that we had died when our brethren died before the LORD! Why have you brought the assembly of the LORD into this wilderness, that we should die here, both we and our cattle? And why have you made us come up out of Egypt, to bring us to this evil place? It is no place for grain, or figs, or vines, or pomegranates; and there is no water to drink." Then Moses and Aaron went from the presence of the assembly to the door of the tent of meeting, and fell on their faces. And the glory of the LORD appeared to them, and the LORD said to Moses, "Take the rod, and assemble the congregation, you and Aaron your brother, and tell the rock before

---

employment of incantations, spells, and formula (pronounced words) united to certain bits of matter (hemlock, chicken bones, herbs, etc.) are parodies on the sacraments whose words are only efficacious because of their union with the Word. Hence, words like *hocus pocus* were a mockery of *hoc est enim corpus meum* of the Holy Mass. Magic as such did not prove effective. It now is in some sense the opposite of sacraments. Sacraments do not "look" like what they in fact are whereas magic attempts to trick the eye into seeing what is not.

their eyes to yield its water; so you shall bring water out of the rock for them; so you shall give drink to the congregation and their cattle." And Moses took the rod from before the LORD, as he commanded him.

And Moses and Aaron gathered the assembly together before the rock, and he said to them, "Hear now, you rebels; shall we bring forth water for you out of this rock?" And Moses lifted up his hand and struck the rock with his rod twice; and water came forth abundantly, and the congregation drank, and their cattle. And the LORD said to Moses and Aaron, "Because you did not believe in me, to sanctify me in the eyes of the people of Israel, therefore you shall not bring this assembly into the land which I have given them." (Nm 20:2–12)[6]

Moses struck the rock, as he had before, and water came forth. What did he do wrong? In Exodus 17 he struck the rock and all who were thirsty were given to drink. Now he strikes the rock, albeit twice, and while the Israelites drink, he receives a punishment.

A central theme in all of Scripture is fidelity to the word of God. Moses was not asked to strike the rock, *but to speak to the rock*. What a curious command. Understood, however, in light of Christ, as all of Scripture must be, it is quite profound. St. Paul states in reference to the people of Israel, that they "all drank the same supernatural drink. For they drank from the supernatural Rock which followed them, and the Rock was Christ" (1 Cor 10:4). Christ is the rock. Christ is the rock

---

6   The importance of this passage was brought to my attention reading *Sacraments in Scripture* by Tim Gray. Cf. *Catechism of the Catholic Church,* nos. 1366–67.

who was struck on Golgotha to give us living water. This sacrifice is not repeated. Christ is never sacrificed (struck) again. The Letter to the Hebrews states:

> "Sacrifices and offerings you have not desired,
> but a body you have prepared for me;
> in burnt offerings and sin offerings you have taken
>   no pleasure.
> Then I said, 'Behold, I have come to do your will, O
>   God,'
> as it is written of me in the roll of the book."
>
> When he said above, "You have neither desired nor taken pleasure in sacrifices and offerings and burnt offerings and sin offerings" (these are offered according to the law), then he added, "Behold, I have come to do your will." He abolishes the first in order to establish the second. And by that will we have been sanctified through the offering of the body of Jesus Christ once for all." (Heb 10:5–10)

Christ is never struck again. The act which brings forth the fruit of that sacrifice is enacted by a word. The priest speaks to the Rock, as it were, pronouncing *to* matter. That matter pours forth, like water from a rock, the grace that has been commanded. This is a sacrament. Christ's power comes to us in the sacraments. In the words of the Fathers of the Church, this water from the rock, this power from Christ, comes to us through material signs like water is transported through an aqueduct. Christ's power is called a *vis fluens*, a "flowing power," coming to us from his Divinity by means of his humanity employing a further material instrument (bread, water, oil, et cetera).

THE TASSEL AND THE TOUCH

This flowing power can be seen clearly in the eighth chapter of Luke:

> And a woman who had had a flow of blood for twelve years and had spent all her living upon physicians and could not be healed by any one, came up behind him, and touched the fringe of his garment; and immediately her flow of blood ceased. And Jesus said, "Who was it that touched me?" When all denied it, Peter said, "Master, the multitudes surround you and press upon you!" But Jesus said, "Some one touched me; for I perceive that power has gone forth from me." And when the woman saw that she was not hidden, she came trembling, and falling down before him declared in the presence of all the people why she had touched him, and how she had been immediately healed. And he said to her, "Daughter, your faith has made you well; go in peace." (Lk 8:43–48)

"Who touched me?" What caused Our Lord to say this? The text tells us. He perceived that power had gone out of him, almost as if it had been stolen. We will return to this passage later to discuss our fruitful participation in the sacraments. For now, this passage perfectly explains what was said above: Divine power alone can heal. Yet this power comes through the humanity of Christ extending even to a tassel on his garment.

VISIBLE AND AUDIBLE SIGNS TO INVISIBLE GRACE SIGNIFIED

St. Thomas Aquinas once noted that you and I learn best by moving from what is more known to what is less known. We are literally "at home" in matter. We are not angels. We were not meant to exist without bodies. We are composite beings, made of body and soul.

Furthermore, we know things abstractly by means of material things. When a teacher speaks about concepts directly, we strain to understand. The higher the concept, the quicker we are to feel confusion. We want to "imagine" the thing, which is simply another way of reducing the concept to something material. When the teacher finally says, "Let me give you an example," we all sigh in relief knowing that the concept will take on flesh; it will be placed in matter. We may lose something in the transition of pure concept to something concrete, but we feel more at home and get a foothold. Once we are intellectually steady we are ready once again to try to reach up.

This is the reason that we employ such things as metaphor. When we see something "which lies too deep for words,"[7] we clothe it in symbolic material imagery. Thus, it is that material reality which signifies various concepts for us. Matter itself is symbolic. I noted earlier that words are material signs that convey a concept or an idea. The material is a sort of vehicle for the spiritual. If I want to say that I love you, I could do so in as many languages as I know, each having different "matter" but conveying the same concept. Other material things do this as well. As just one example, in an emoji age, instead

---

7   *Intimations of Immortality,* William Wordsworth.

of saying I love you, one could just text a red heart to convey the same meaning. It may be a bit vaguer, but the concept is the same.

The medievals used to speak of the Book of Scripture and the Book of Nature as two sources of Divine Revelation. In other words, God reveals himself in creation as well as in the inspired text. St. Paul affirms this in his letter to the Romans, stating: "Ever since the creation of the world his invisible nature, namely, his eternal power and deity, has been clearly perceived in the things that have been made" (Rom 1:20).

All creation resembles God to some degree as an effect resembles its cause. What we see further in the Scriptures, however, is that God, as the Lord of history, as the Alpha and the Omega, can employ not just words but persons, places, and things to indicate a further meaning. We call this *typology*. Namely, things in the Old Testament (as in the rock example of Numbers) mean something in their own time and place, but also something more in the full revelation of Christ. On the road to Emmaus, Christ interprets the entirety of the Old Testament as having its full meaning only in him.

In a similar way, the sacraments employ matter which have a symbolic meaning, and yet, with the words or formula that is added to them, a further signification is given to them. Sacraments have both something material as well as verbal, a "formula." They each signify something. The verbal sign gives a further signification to the material sign.

For example, water has classically been a symbol both of life and of death. I cannot live without it and yet I cannot control it. It is powerful and necessary, yet the absence or the presence of it may cause death. Furthermore, it is also that which when used cleanses the body of filth. These three natural significations are thus naturally known. Unlike words, they are natural signs, not conventional. Every society in every age understands them without explication even if the languages in each of those societies have different modalities to express the reality of "water."

Thus, the sacrament of Baptism employs these natural significations: life, death, and cleansing. Yet, when God's word is united to the water, "I baptize you in the name of the Father, and of the Son and of the Holy Spirit," something further is signified. St. Augustine says water touches the body but the heart is what is cleansed. In other words, life, death, and cleansing do take place but not for the body. The soul of man undergoes a radical change, participating in the death of Christ and born to new life, cleansed of all sin.

This is why the sacraments are called "efficacious signs." The sacraments effect what they signify. They signify by both the material employed by God (water) and the further signification of the words God employs through his agent (minister). The reason I liken all of this to biblical typology is that God's material creation has a further signification we had not known prior to the New Covenant. There is something so simple and humble about water, bread, wine, and oil, but what dignity and nobility they have been raised to! When God made these realities and man employed his intelligence to raise them higher (in the case of bread, wine, and oil), he had his Son's Body and Blood in mind; he had the Holy Spirit in mind.

Finally, what is done? Christ's power flows from his Divinity through his humanity and touches, by means of the physical/spiritual composite of matter and words, the individual recipient. Since Christ is the principle agent, the Church teaches that the sacraments are always efficacious. Given that the proper form (words) and matter are employed by the proper minister (living instrumental agent), the sacraments work *ex opere operato*, from the work worked. This means simply that they receive their efficacy (their usefulness) from Christ's power, not the merit of the recipient. For them to be fruitful in us is a different question.

OUR FRUITFUL USE OF THE SACRAMENTS

Recall the passage of the woman with a terrible hemorrhage. Many were touching our Lord, so thick was the crowd, but only one was touched by him. The difference, Christ tells us, was her faith. But what is faith?

Most things that we "know" in life we hold either on the authority of another or as an opinion. When we don't see things either for ourselves or else clearly enough to "know," we have belief or opinion. The mind rests when it sees something. It grasps hold of its object and "comprehends." I do not have the opinion that two and two equal four. I see it. My mother does not believe that she is my mother, she knows it. When the mind does not have this clarity of sight, it can only adhere to a conclusion by assistance from our will. I choose to adhere to a conclusion (even though I may be wrong).

Faith is like this insofar as it adheres firmly to something it does not yet fully see. We walk by faith, St. Paul says, not by sight (2 Cor 5:7). Yet unlike simple belief or opinion, the will is aided by grace to move the intellect's adherence. In other words, God is the primary cause of faith in himself. We cannot cause it. Have you ever noticed that you cannot give someone faith? You can only argue that the truths of the Faith are in accordance with reason. To adhere firmly to God's revelation in Jesus Christ is a virtue given to us by the Holy Spirit. We must pray for it.

Faith is in some sense the keeping of his word. The woman with the hemorrhage had this gift. She adhered tightly to his word and thus knew that power was in him and would come forth from him. Still greater than this woman is the Blessed Mother, outside of whom there has never been a more perfect or willing recipient of Divine grace. Indeed, she is spoken of by Christ as blessed *because* she heard the word of God and kept it (Lk 11:28).

I mentioned that the Annunciation is an analogy for all of the sacraments. She hears the word of God, she adheres to the word of God, she maintains the word of God, and the Word of God dwells in her. Christ said clearly: "If you love me, you will keep my commandments" (Jn 14:15). Further, he states: "If a man loves me, he will keep my word, and my Father will love him, and we will come to him and make our home with him" (Jn 14:23).

The purposes of the Incarnation are to reveal, to redeem, and to give us access to Divine life. The sacraments are the means by which this action of Christ is applied to us from the Incarnation. They reveal his sacred action by their signification; they apply the redemptive action of Christ and give us participation in Divine life. The extent to which that Divine life grows in us is also dependent, however, on the keeping of his commandments, the maintaining of his Word. We cannot cast him out and expect to grow in his life. Faith, this firm adherence to him, draws deeper and deeper power. The prime example of this is the Blessed Mother.

The objectivity of Christ's actions in the sacraments means that I don't have to live on fragile ground with him. I don't have to question whether he will give me his life, his power. I need not doubt whether he will forgive me, whether he will take an ordinary man and make him his intimate in action by grace. He always keeps his word. The question in the sacraments is whether *I* will keep his word.

THE EFFECTS OF THE SACRAMENTS

When the sacraments reach their end or fruition, what do they accomplish? If the sacraments are Christ's work, what do they do? We will go through each one individually, but it's helpful to make some distinctions now that will serve us throughout the rest of our investigation.

We can break sacraments down into three movements or effects: 1) significations, 2) significations and grace together, and 3) the grace that remains when the signs are gone.[8]

As always, let us look at the actions of our Lord to give us historical examples. In the ninth chapter of St. John's Gospel, we read:

> As he [Jesus] passed by, he saw a man blind from his birth. And his disciples asked him, "Rabbi, who sinned, this man or his parents, that he was born blind?" Jesus answered, "It was not that this man sinned, or his parents, but that the works of God might be made manifest in him. We must work the works of him

---

[8]   The medievals described this tripartite reality of each sacrament as *sacramentum tantum* (sacrament or sign alone), *sacramentum et res* (sign and reality/grace together) as immediate effect, *res tantum* (reality/grace alone) ultimate effect.

who sent me, while it is day; night comes, when no one can work. As long as I am in the world, I am the light of the world." As he said this, he spat on the ground and made clay of the spittle and anointed the man's eyes with the clay, saying to him, "Go, wash in the pool of Silo´am" (which means Sent). So he went and washed and came back seeing. The neighbors and those who had seen him before as a beggar, said, "Is not this the man who used to sit and beg?" Some said, "It is he"; others said, "No, but he is like him." He said, "I am the man." They said to him, "Then how were your eyes opened?" He answered, "The man called Jesus made clay and anointed my eyes and said to me, 'Go to Silo´am and wash'; so I went and washed and received my sight." (Jn 9:1–11)

What we see in this passage is the triple movement of the sacraments. There is the sign, which is clay made with spittle, and the words, "Go and wash." This intimate action of our Lord refashioning a man's eyes out of clay brings to mind God's action in the second creation account in Genesis. There, God himself forms man. Here, the Godman repairs man. While this sign is administered, something else happens, namely, the reality of his restored sight. But he does not know this until he washes. Once he does, there is no longer a sign, there is simply sight. This sight continues even when the sign of healing, the clay, is no longer on his eyes. It is the ultimate effect of Christ's action, that the man see, and ultimately that the man see Christ himself: "Jesus heard that they had cast him out, and having found him he said, 'Do you believe in the Son of man?' He answered, 'And who is he, sir, that I may believe in him?' Jesus said to him, 'You have seen him, and it is he who speaks to you.' He said, 'Lord, I believe'; and he worshiped him" (Jn 9:35–38).

The man blind from birth saw what his eyes were made to see: Jesus Christ.

CHAPTER 2

SACRAMENT OF DIVINE LIFE: BAPTISM

GROWTH IN DIVINE LIFE LIKENED TO GROWTH IN THE BODY

All religions have natural sacraments. While their various signs might point to significant events, they are not *efficacious signs*. Meaning, they do not effect what they signify. Sociologically speaking, these rites often coincide with both individual and communal growth. The seven sacraments differ in that they are principally actions of Jesus Christ rather than the individual or community. They differ in that they effect what they signify. They differ in that it is not human growth they foster and celebrate but growth in Divine life. Yet they are similar in that just as the body individually and communally goes through various stages in human life, so too are we given grace which corresponds to growth (individually and communally) in Divine life.

When asking about the number of the sacraments, St. Thomas Aquinas uses this analogy to bodily growth:

Now a man attains perfection in the corporeal life in two ways: first, in regard to his own person; secondly, in regard to the whole community of the society in which he lives, for man is by nature a social animal. With regard to himself man is perfected in the life of the body, in two ways; first, directly, i.e. by acquiring some vital perfection; secondly, indirectly, i.e. by the removal of hindrances to life, such as ailments, or the like. Now the life of the body is perfected "directly," in three ways. First, by generation whereby a man begins to be and to live: and corresponding to this in the spiritual life there is Baptism, which is a spiritual regeneration, according to Titus 3:5: "By the laver of regeneration," etc. Secondly, by growth whereby a man is brought to perfect size and strength: and corresponding to this in the spiritual life there is Confirmation, in which the Holy Spirit is given to strengthen us. Wherefore the disciples who were already baptized were bidden thus: "Stay you in the city till you be endued with power from on high" (Lk. 24:49). Thirdly, by nourishment, whereby life and strength are preserved to man; and corresponding to this in the spiritual life there is the Eucharist. Wherefore it is said (Jn. 6:54): "Except you eat of the flesh of the Son of Man, and drink His blood, you shall not have life in you."

And this would be enough for man if he had an impassible life [incapable of suffering], both corporally and spiritually; but since man is liable at times to both corporal and spiritual infirmity, i.e. sin, hence man needs a cure from his infirmity; which cure is twofold. One is the healing, that restores health: and corresponding to this in the spiritual life there is Penance, according to Ps. 40:5: "Heal my soul, for I have sinned against Thee." The other is the restoration of former vigor by means of suitable diet and exercise: and corresponding to this in the spiritual life there is Extreme Unction, which removes the remainder of sin, and prepares man for final glory. Wherefore it is written (James 5:15): "And if he be in sins they shall be forgiven him."

In regard to the whole community, man is perfected in two ways. First, by receiving power to rule the community and to exercise public acts: and corresponding to this in the spiritual life there is the sacrament of order, according to the saying of Heb. 7:27, that priests offer sacrifices not for themselves only, but also for the people. Secondly in regard to natural propagation. This is accomplished by Matrimony both in the corporal and in the spiritual life: since it is not only a sacrament but also a function of nature."[9]

Far from being simply a sociological phenomenon, God, who in his Divine Wisdom created the stages of the body, imitates what he created by stages of growth in the Mystical Body of his Church. It is impossible to speak about growth and healing, however, if we do not first have life. All that St. Thomas mentions is predicated on the gift of existence and being born. So, too, we must, as Christ taught us, be born again.

---

[9] *Summa Theologiae,* III, q. 65 a. 1 c.

Being Born From Above

Baptism is the door of Divine life. Christ commanded his Apostles to baptize all nations in the name of the Father, and of the Son, and of the Holy Spirit (see Mt 28:19). In speaking with Nicodemus much earlier, Christ said that we had to be born *again*. That word also means "from above" (*anothen*), therefore both senses of the word are true. When I am born, I have a nature, as we said above. Indeed, the very word *nature* comes from the Latin word meaning "to be born" (*natus*).

What am I born with? Do I come into the world with a human nature? Yes. Do I come into the world with a Divine nature? No. We call someone father or mother because from them we received our human nature. But how do we call God Father if we do not have his nature? In a loose sense, we are able to call him Father because our human nature also comes from him as our Creator. But we cannot call God Father in the true sense of having received his nature, unless by adoptive sonship. What being born "again" from "above" does is usher us into Divine participation. About this new spirit that we receive, St. Paul says: "For you did not receive the spirit of slavery to fall back into fear, but you have received the spirit of sonship. When we cry, 'Abba! Father!'" (Rom 8:15).

Once we possess this Divine life, we are then open to receive all of the sacraments which operate on that life, as St. Thomas noted in that lengthy passage. Why are other sacraments necessary? As Thomas further notes, because, analogous to bodily and communal life, the nascent life received is like a newborn infant. The first Sunday after Easter was called *Quasimodo infantes* because the new Christians, having been baptized on Easter, were "like infants." For eight days they were required to wear their baptismal garments and stay in the protective care of the bishop who would further instruct them. On the eighth day, the day of re-creation, they were allowed to remove their white robes and go into the world.

The divine life of grace at the infant stage is small and fragile. It needs growth and strength like any newborn. This requires our cooperation. As St. Augustine once noted, God created us without us, but he will not save us without us. Nor will he save us as individuals. Just as an infant must be cared for by his or her parents, so too the *neophyte* (new nature in Greek) must be cared for by Mother Church with instruction and sustenance, protected and guided, and allowed to flourish in the growth of grace.

The image of the infant highlights the personal nature or reciprocity of the sacrament. I mentioned that the sacrament is efficacious because of Christ's action, but in some sense, that is only half the story. An infant must receive care, be able to digest food, and keep sickness at bay. This aspect of receptivity changes as he grows. As the child's mind develops and he asks questions about purpose, he directs himself to certain ends and chooses one good over another good. He must choose to receive something. Everyone knows that outside of physical force, with violence or threat of punishment, one cannot *make* a child eat spinach. You are a rational creature endowed with faculties which make you a type of lord over your own actions. This personal element of response is part of the sacraments.[10]

---

[10]   The Church notes that this passive or active receptive disposition of the recipient is necessary for God's gift to bear fruit.

Elements of the Sacrament

Christ said to Nicodemus that we must be born of water and the Spirit. Water is a natural sign to which is added the words "I baptize you . . ." It is a sign of life, death, and purification. The Scriptures are replete with imagery to show how water has been symbolic in the Old Testament, pointing to its ultimate sense in the New Covenant. The blessing of water before Baptism poetically mentions three Divine usages of this humble and essential element:

> Father, you give us grace through sacramental signs, which tell us of the wonders of your unseen power. In baptism we use your gift of water, which you have made a rich symbol of the grace you give us in this sacrament. At the very dawn of creation your spirit breathed on the waters, making them the wellspring of all holiness. The waters of the great flood you made a sign of the waters of baptism that make an end of sin and a new beginning of goodness. Through the waters of the Red Sea you led Israel out of slavery. To be an image of God's holy people, set free from sin by baptism.

The first image of the Holy Spirit "hovering" over the waters in creation is a sign that waters belong to him and he will use it to give life. The other two images link water with life, but also with death. In this sacrament, both death and life are signified as well. St. Paul teaches that in baptism we are plunged into Christ's death (see Rom 6:3). The baptism of Christ's death for which he longed (Lk 12:50) would be shared in by those who were his followers (Mk 10:38). In this baptism, we are purified of sin. The "old man" in us receives a deathblow and the new man begins to live. If we have died with him, we begin to rise with him. Christ plunged himself into the waters of the Jordan as he plunged himself into the sin of man in the Baptism of his Crucifixion. We are submerged in his death by the washing of Baptism.

Thus, the material element of Baptism is water and the form is taken directly from Sacred Scripture: I baptize you in the name of the Father and of the Son and of the Holy Spirit. This three-fold invocation is curious. In the imparting of a new nature, we do not say I baptize you in the name of God. Nor do we say I baptize you in the name of Jesus Christ. Baptism administered in the Trinitarian formula richly manifests that the life in which we participate is a Trinitarian life. The nature is Divine and yet the Persons in whom we live and move and have our new being are three, equal in majesty, perfect in unity. When we say Jesus Christ, we are specifically saying God saves (the name Jesus means precisely this) through the Christ (the anointed one) to rend (open) the heavens (as happened at his own baptism and at his death) which gives us access to Trinitarian life.

It is proper to the priest to administer this sacrament, which is why we call him Father. He instrumentally causes Divine life in us. Yet such is the nature of this sacrament, such is its importance, that in the case of an emergency anyone is permitted to administer it, provided that person does what the Church herself intends and there is water present. Thus, deacons often baptize and in emergencies anyone may licitly do so.

EFFECTS OF THE SACRAMENT

A priest friend of mine was newly ordained when he encountered a rather significant and unusual problem. He was teaching the children in his parish who were preparing for First Holy Communion. That is not usually a difficult crowd. Few objections are raised at that age and no real challenges are levied against the teaching. Yet, on this occasion, one of the children was adamant that he did not believe in the Real Presence of Christ in the Eucharist. What seemed at first just a precocious defiance turned into a manifestation of genuine disbelief.

On the one hand, my friend could have discussed all of the niceties of Eucharistic doctrine—scripturally, metaphysically, historically, and liturgically—but that didn't seem to be quite appropriate for a seven-year-old. He mentioned the case to his pastor. The elder man responded: "Check and make sure he was baptized." As it turned out, the child had not, in fact, been baptized. After some preparation, the child was duly baptized.

What do you suppose happened? You guessed it! Once he had received the grace of this sacrament, the child himself asked to receive Holy Communion, professing belief in the true Body and Blood of Christ in the Eucharist.

What happened in this case? It speaks to the effects of the sacrament and to the fruitful participation in it. I noted that we are rational creatures. We have a *life* that is rational. We call this rational life the soul. A new life principle is given to the soul in Baptism called sanctifying grace. This is Divine life begun in us. I used the analogy of an infant who grows up and, as he grows, his faculties develop. He doesn't just have "rational life." He begins to use his powers or faculties that grow from that life, namely, to think and to will, to know and to love. As grace is a new principle of Divine life in the soul, so too out of grace grows three virtues which assist our knowing and loving. These virtues are called theological because they are potent capacities which come from God and lead to God. Faith is given to perfect our intellect (perfect our knowing) while hope and charity are given to perfect our will (perfect our loving).

In the case I described, the child did not have this principle of grace inside of him. As a result of this absence of grace, he did not have the theological virtues either. He simply *could not* believe in the Eucharist. Once the grace of Baptism was given to him, he began to see. Faith was operative in his mind, allowing him to adhere to what Christ had revealed about the gift of his Body and Blood as food and drink. Rare is it that we see grace and the virtues in such incredible contrast with their absence. They are usually rather subtle in their activity. Nevertheless, no one can say Jesus is Lord except by the power of the Holy Spirit (1 Cor 12:3). Baptism is new life flourishing in us, fruitful even unto the powers or faculties of the soul.

CHARACTER

When we first meet someone, we quickly become cognizant of his or her character. Are those we meet pleasant or grumpy? Are they shy or gregarious? Do they have a strong moral character or are they prone to deceit and malice? Are they generous or greedy?

The word *character* comes from a Greek word meaning

an engraved mark or sign. A soldier or slave, for example, was stamped or branded. Three sacraments impart to us a certain character that is irrevocable: Baptism, Confirmation, and Holy Orders. The word *character* is used in the Letter to the Hebrews in speaking of the Son's coequality with the Father: "He reflects the glory of God and bears the very stamp of his nature, upholding the universe by his word of power" (Heb 1:3). Another word employed to describe this character is *seal*. God, St. Paul states, has put his seal upon us (see 2 Cor 1:22).[11]

What does this character or seal do to the soul? Recall that a sacrament, like an aqueduct, has a certain transitory nature. The power of God flows through it. Recall also that in the sacrament of Baptism what remains in the soul after sacramental washing and cleansing of sin is the reality of sanctifying grace and virtues. This new life remains in the soul despite the fact that the holy water is now dried and gone and everyone has left the church building (just like, you may recall, the clay was gone and washed away from the man's eyes but his ability to see remained).

In addition to this reality, something more is given, and that is a certain consecration and configuration for Divine worship. There is a "character" imparted at Baptism. One can lose the grace newly received by serious sin. One can lose the virtues which grow like shoots from the soil of that

---

[11]   The seal is a symbol close to that of anointing. "The Father has set his seal" on Christ and also seals us in him. Because this seal indicates the indelible effect of the anointing with the Holy Spirit in the sacraments of Baptism, Confirmation, and Holy Orders, the image of the seal (*sphragis*) has been used in some theological traditions to express the indelible "character" imprinted by these three unrepeatable sacraments. *Catechism of the Catholic Church*, no. 698. See ibid., no. 1121.

grace. Have you ever heard of someone "losing" their faith? It doesn't happen the way one loses keys, by absentmindedness.[12] One cannot lose a character. The soul is marked, sealed, and consecrated to worship in Spirit and in truth (Jn 4:24). Sacramental character disposes us as a certain kind of power to receive or to bestow gifts on others that pertain to true worship. The indelible nature of this character is the very reason we can return to the Church by sacramental confession. We have the character of Baptism to "receive" the gift of Christ's priestly mediation of mercy. More than simply a negative, however, this character not only directs us to receive the grace we had lost but orients us toward Holy Communion. It opens the soul to desire for and to receive Christ's consummate gift of himself in the Holy Eucharist (like the little boy I told you about).

FRUITFULNESS OF THE SACRAMENT

A principle we saw in the beginning pertaining to fruitfulness is fidelity to the Word. In common vernacular, we say that someone is a man of his word, or that she has kept her word. In the life of the sacraments, we must keep *his* word. What does this mean?

First, in our baptismal promises, we confessed that we reject Satan, his deceits, his works, and his empty promises. Satan is a liar and the father of lies. The keeping of his word and the rejection of God's word was the cause of our downfall. Whose word do we now keep? Are we informed as to the

---

[12]   I will return to this topic in the discussion of the sacrament of Penance.

truth of reality by reason and faith or do we adhere to the serpentine susurrations of society.

Furthermore, in our baptismal promises, we professed the creed and adherence to all that God has revealed. We promised to keep his word. Have we done so? If not, why not? What are those things which habitually fracture our friendship with him? Which relationship, which habit, which fear attacks the new life in us, coiling around our faith, depleting our hope, and choking our charity? What measures do we take to maintain his word? Do we pray? Do we meditate on his Word in Sacred Scripture?

Finally, the rest of this book will have to do with the way in which the other sacraments give the grace to complete and fulfill that which was begun in Baptism. In short, if we are living with Baptism alone, we are living a half-life that awaits further completion.

In the ancient baptismal rite, the catechumen was instructed to spit in the direction of Satan and of his old life before descending into the baptismal waters. He is immersed in the waters, baptized, and comes out on the other side of the font. The image is of one descending into Christ's death and rising to new life with him. While perhaps not as dramatic a gesture, the same was done by us at our baptism. The new life we received was symbolically clothed with a white garment as a sign of our purity and a flaming candle was given to us signifying the light by which we live. This light is Christ, the truth himself who now informs our mind with faith. This new life, as noted, was young and fresh but also fragile in its nascence. It needed to grow and be strengthened. Growth is a cooperative act, both divine and human.

Two sacraments, however, are given to us to assist in this

growth, and one in particular to which all the sacraments tend. The first is Confirmation and the second is the Most Holy Eucharist. These three make up what are called the "sacraments of initiation." To possess all three is to *begin* the process of divinization, but not necessarily to finish. "Incorporation" into his mystical body occurs when the lifeblood of his grace flows into us. We are grafted onto him and must have the "sap" of the vine flowing through us to live and bear fruit. Without him, we can do nothing. To participate perfectly in this life requires actively receiving and yielding to the work of that grace in us.

Finally, if the character of Baptism enables us to participate in proper worship, this means that we enter into the passion of our Lord and his Eucharistic sacrifice. The fulfillment of Baptism—Baptism brought to fruition—will only truly occur when I have offered myself perfectly to the Father through the offering of the Son.

CHAPTER 3

SACRAMENT OF DIVINE LIFE STRENGTHENED: CONFIRMATION

SEALED WITH THE GIFT OF THE HOLY SPIRIT

What is the sacrament of Confirmation? Again, we must turn to the Sacred Scriptures to get our bearings. When Christ was baptized in the Jordan, the Holy Spirit descended upon Jesus and confirmed him as the anointed one. Immediately following this, the Spirit thrust Jesus into the desert. The word employed, *ekballo*, literally means "to throw out" (see Mk 1:10–12). The Holy Spirit threw Christ into the desert? What is this force? What is this compulsion?

The impression or impulse of the Holy Spirit is one of strengthening. Christ is fortified. Why? He goes into the desert for two main reasons: 1) to prepare for his public ministry and 2) to grapple with Satan through prayer, fasting, and temptation. Up until this time, Christ had lived in the silent

44

solitude of Nazareth. Now he was to speak, to give his word by which he would capture souls as a man catches fish in a net. When that word met resistance and refusal, it would entail battle. When that word was received, salvation for the recipient ensued. Strength was needed.

We can easily think of scenes from the Gospels in which enemies of Christ attempted to seize him, stone him, cast him off a cliff. These scenes showcase the amazing power and restraint of Christ, manifested as he "walked through the midst of them" without harm. Yet we often forget the level of endurance necessary for Christ to give himself so tire- lessly. How often, for example, do the Scriptures relate that the "whole town" came to him for healing, that he spent the night in prayer after an entire day of self-sacrifice, that even in the wilderness thousands crowded around him or dropped an invalid down through a roof. Christ had gone out to the desert to prepare for three years of exhaustive donation. Commenting on the baptism, anointing, and preparation of Christ, St. Luke states that he returned "in the power of the Spirit" (Lk 4:14).

Where were the Apostles in relation to this power? How often they were fatigued and fell asleep. How often they com- plained about the crowds. How often they were fearful of reproach, suffering, and death. This fear mounted to climactic heights causing them all to abandon and deny their Savior. One only remained and was a witness to his passion.

Before his ascension, Christ promised his Apostles that he would clothe them with power from on High. This power was the giving of His Spirit: "'And behold, I send the prom- ise of my Father upon you; but stay in the city, until you are clothed with power from on high.' Then he led them out as far as Bethany, and lifting up his hands he blessed them. While he blessed them, he parted from them and was carried up into heaven. And they worshipped him, and returned to Jerusalem with great joy, and were continually in the temple blessing God" (Lk 24:49–53).

They are filled with joy. The promise is coming. The confirmation. They will be "with strength." When the Spirit descends upon them at Pentecost, they are indeed clothed with power. Different men they are with such power. They are no longer content to linger in the silent solitude of the upper room. The word they had received was not simply for them. They were to preach to all nations. Huddled in expectant prayer, they waited in the company of the woman who knew what was to befall them, for she had been clothed long ago in this Spirit. The rush of wind came, blew like a bellow into their souls. Tongues of fire burned the bands which bound their tongues, and they began to preach. It would be received by some. It would be rejected by many. For this word they would suffer, but never again would they forsake his word. They were powerful. They had been strengthened.

MATURE IN CHRIST

Baptism and Confirmation correspond roughly to personal sanctification and communal sanctification. The Holy Spirit is given in Baptism making us sons and daughters in the Son. In Confirmation, however, he strengthens us for the building up of the Body of Christ. Confirmation, as seen in the life of our Lord and with his Apostles, clothes us with power for fortitude in battle, endurance in trial, and generous sacrifice to "preach the Word in season and out of season" (2 Tm 2:4).

Christ was approximately thirty years old when the Spirit drove him into the desert. The Apostles were not children. This is a sign of the growth in spiritual maturity that takes place. Children do not have responsibility for the care of their parents. But as they grow, their sphere of responsibility is extended. So too in the Mystical Body. I am not concerned simply with my personal relationship with Jesus. I am part of a Body. I am strengthened to build up that Body. Think of how one member of our physical bodies will bear more to assist a lame limb. If my sight is impaired, my other senses come to the ready. If my left ankle is sprained, my right must bear the burden. If I am cold, my extremities must sacrifice their blood to protect the internal organs. No part of a body lives for itself. Dissension in a body is disintegration. It is ultimately death. St. Paul goes so far as to proclaim, "Now I rejoice in my sufferings for your sake, and in my flesh I complete what is lacking in Christ's afflictions for the sake of his body, that is, the Church" (Col 1:24). Further, St. Paul states that he himself labors to preach Christ, "Him we proclaim, warning every man and teaching every man in all wisdom, that we may present every man mature in Christ" (Col 1:28).

ELEMENTS OF THE SACRAMENT

Confirmation is administered by the bishop (or his delegate) since he is a successor of the Apostles. The very mitre he wears in liturgical ceremonies is a reminder and sign of the tongues of fire which hovered over the heads of the Apostles. He administers the sign by the laying on of hands and the anointing with *chrism*. The words spoken are, "Be sealed with the gift of the Holy Spirit. Peace be with you." As he pronounces these words, a cross is traced on the forehead. What do these significations mean?

First, as we shall see, the ceremonial "laying on of hands" by priests in ancient Israel was a sign of sacrifice. The priests laid hands on animals which were marked out for sacrifice, imposing the sins of the people upon them and marking them out as offered to the Lord. This sacrificial overtone is present in Confirmation, marking one out as an offering for others. Second, chrism takes its name from Christ, the Anointed one. The candidate is signed with the cross, for God's elect bear his name on their foreheads (see Rv 22:4) as they bravely enter into sacrifice. They are "sealed." As we saw, this is the imparting of a character which cannot be removed. The confirmed are oriented to offer themselves in union with the priesthood of Christ by their participation in the sacrifice of praise. This capacity endures forever.

EFFECTS OF THE SACRAMENT

The effects of the sacrament can be clearly seen from the explanation above. The divine life in us is strengthened to witness to Christ in word and in deed. In addition to the signification of form whereby we are sealed by the Holy Spirit, the bishop invokes the gifts of the Holy Spirit present to us in Baptism but now directed to this witness: "All powerful God, Father of our Lord Jesus Christ, by water and the Holy Spirit you freed your sons and daughters from sin and gave them new life. Send your Holy Spirit upon them to be their helper and guide. Give them the spirit of wisdom and understanding, the spirit of right judgment and courage, the spirit of knowledge and reverence. Fill them with the spirit of wonder and awe in your presence. We ask this through Christ our Lord" (From the Bishop's Missal).

While all of these gifts are necessary and employed in the witness we must give, one of them is most fitting to the sacrament by the very name of *confirmation*: "courage" or "fortitude." But what exactly is supernatural fortitude?

EVER-VIRGIN MARY AS THE FRUITION OF SUPERNATURAL FORTITUDE

In the great fortress convent of Santa Chiara, perched above the Umbrian valley, women known as the Poor Clares have manned their stations for nine hundred years. I choose words like *fortress* and *manned* deliberately as you will see. One of the aged nuns was recently giving me some advice. In 2016, after a few years of labor, our bishop formally erected a new seminary in our diocese and appointed me as rector. With excitement, a touch of wonder, and no doubt a pinch of pride, I was recounting to her how many fine young men we have in our newly established seminary. Given the state of vocations in Italy, I admit that I expected her to glow with admiration. Instead, she shook her head as if shaking my very security, squeezed my hand to fortify me, and said, "*Ma manca la resistenza-insegna la perseveranza.*" These words from a religious of seventy years echoing in a basilica which has seen the coming and going of countless vocations could not fail to reverberate in the youthfulness of our endeavor. She was right. "What is missing is strength, we must teach perseverance."

Vocations there are, always have been, always will be. What is lacking these days is the courage which manifests itself not only in the initial bestowal but above all in the strength of endurance. We must, as she commanded, teach perseverance in all vocations. How can we be mature in Christ, witness to Christ, if we flee in the midst of battle or surrender to the onslaught of evil? We need fortitude. We need the fruitful exercise of the sacrament of Confirmation.

Vespers in the seminary is sung with varying solemnity depending on the grade of the feast. For solemn vespers, we employ the Church's *antiphonale romanum*, which is the Liturgy of the Hours set to Gregorian chant for the singing of the Office. We were in seminary but a week when we celebrated the feast of the Assumption. The first antiphon for Solemn Vespers struck me for a number of reasons.

First, because I had never seen it before as applied to Our Lady in the liturgy. Context sometimes makes things stand out in stark relief. I had never seen it in the liturgy because it has been removed from the breviary. It was in the breviary (the prayer book of the priest) prayed before the Second Vatican Council. It exists now only in the sung version of vespers. The new antiphon you find in the breviary describes Christ ascending into the heavens.

Why was the old one removed? I do not know, but perhaps it is precisely because of its militant content. However, keeping in mind the new one was not pointed for Gregorian chant, it seems that in the sung version the old antiphon remains since it already had musical notation. What seems therefore like liturgical laziness is ironically emblematic of what is lacking in the state of vocations. This will become evident when you see the antiphon.

The liturgy is replete with passages about Our Lady's faith, her beauty, her purity, and her grace. What we have been sorely lacking in our vision is her strength. Here is the antiphon which had been applied to Our Lady, first in the Latin and then in its translation. It is a passage from the Song of Songs, chapter six, verse nine: *quae est ista quae progreditur quasi aurora consurgens pulchra ut luna electa ut sol terribilis ut acies ordinate.* "Who is she who comes forth like the dawn, rising beautiful as the moon, brilliant as the sun, terrible as an army arrayed for battle."

Generations had heard this text applied to Our Lady. The Legion of Mary certainly employed it. Liturgically, however, it is now basically gone. I will apply the entire antiphon to what I consider its fulfillment in the book of Revelation, but first let's consider just that last phrase, so striking as it is to our modern sensibilities: "terrible as an army arrayed for battle."

To begin, let us flip backwards a couple of chapters in the Song of Songs. There we hear the Bridegroom again speaking about the Bride with these words: "Thy neck is like the tower of David built for an armoury, whereon there hang a thousand bucklers, all shields of mighty men" (Sg 4:4).

This, like many comparisons in the Song of Songs, might appear strange. Few women, I imagine, could take it as a grand compliment to have their hair compared to a flock of goats (see Sg 4:1). Yet we must remember that while the Bridegroom is God himself, the Bride is his dwelling place and thus allegorically is described as a city, historically the city of Zion. David's city is the Bride who receives the visitation of the Bridegroom, the place where he dwells. The tower of this city is referred to by the prophet Micah as the place where the King might survey his people (Mi 4:8). The stately ivory tower is wondrous because of its beauty but also because of its formidable strength, so much so that the head himself, the king, might see all from the lofty ramparts. Psalm

48 recalls this awesome sight, adjuring any visitor to the city to: "Walk about Zion, go round about her, / number her towers, / consider well her ramparts, / go through her citadels" (vv. 12–13). She is indeed beautiful, but woe to the one who attempts to besiege her. Her strength is unmatched because it is there that the King dwells.

As the city surrounds the King, so too does a woman encompass her child. Jeremiah's statement that "a woman shall encompass a man" has long been applied to Our Lady (Jer 31:22). She is the true city of God; she is the ark in which he dwells. She encompasses not simply a child but the Son, the Godman in the womb. The Fathers spoke of Our Lady both as the Tower of David and as the neck of the Church over which Christ is the King and Head of his Mystical Body. Thus do we have the application of the Son, the Man, the King who is as "a bridegroom leaving his chamber, / and like a strong man runs its course with joy" (Ps 19:5).

Indeed, the Word entered into this city of Our Lady. He who is the eternally generated *Logos* entered by way of the word. The ancient portals lifted high by her will, the mistress of that city, in an act of faith, allowed the King to enter. He entered, as Ezekiel says, by the East gate, a gate perpetually closed to all others, for only the Lord may enter her. The Virgin is inhabited and her blazing purity is open to him alone. This is the source of her strength. She is the white tower unconquerable to the words of the accuser, the liar from the beginning. The gate is shut and the King dwells therein.

Returning to the antiphon, we also see a discussion of a heavenly host, an army arrayed in front of her for battle. Who is this army? In Genesis we read that at the end of creation, the heavens and the earth were completed as well as all their "hosts" (Gn 2:1; cf Dt 4:19; Is 4:26). It was commonly understood by the ancients that the "hosts of heaven" were akin to the stars in the sky, the army of God. Christ himself makes reference to this as the "fall" of Satan, coming down like lighting from heaven, and St. John adds in the Apocalypse that the dragon (Satan) swept a third of those stars with him in his fall. These are the demons. What of those who remained faithful? The Prophet Baruch has perhaps the most playful and personified of the Divine interactions with the stars. Speaking of God, Baruch states, "He who sends out the light, and it goes, / called it, and it obeyed him in fear; / the stars shone in their watches, and were glad; / he called them, and they said, 'Here we are!' / They shone with gladness for him who made them. / This is our God; / no other can be compared to him!" (Bar 3:33–35).

The connection to the heavenly host and Our Lady is assumed in her title Queen of the Angels. This is an astounding title. By nature inferior and yet by dignity superior! *Vergine Madre, figlia del tuo figlio, umile e alta più che creatura, termine fisso d'etterno consiglio!* More humble and more noble than all creatures, says Dante! Yet what is the image we have in our minds of the angels and Our Lady? The archangel Gabriel, whose very name means "the strength of God," comes to this woman on bended knee. We hear angels ring out the *gloria* after she has given birth. Yet we also have a glimpse in the Apocalypse of a war which took place before she herself was assumed, glorified, and made queen. Michael, the captain of the heavenly host, is sent to her aid. As queen, she becomes the captain of that captain. This image was not lost on the medieval Church.

One striking example of this is found in the glorious

triptych known as the Albrecht Altar outside of Vienna. The panels above the altar depict in form and color the various titles of our Queen. The Queen of the Angels panel is quite curious. In it you see Our Lady as a young girl. Once when I was visiting the monastery of Klosterneuburg, the Fathers there informed me that this image is often mistaken by visitors for St. Joan of Arc. Why? Because the beautiful girl is clad in a blue dress which covers a full suit of armor and breastplate, completed with a wide brimmed hat out of which her long tresses freely fall. She appears to be lifting slightly the hem of her dress to manifest that under such beauty is the armor of strength. She is looking across a tower upon which hang the weapons of the armory. Across the tower are the angels who are seeking an audience with her.

The angels say to her, "Digneris nobiscum sisti/quae turbam daemonum vicisti." (Deign to remain with us, O You who have conquered the horde of demons.)

The Queen of Angels replies, "Ut turris David armis fulta/hic virtute asto multa." (Like the Tower of David, secured with arms on every side, I stand with you in great might.)

Indeed, it is in her that God has shown the strength of his arm, scattering the proud in their conceit. The angels themselves in this depiction seek the aid of their Queen to strengthen them. They are not marveling at her beauty, extolling her purity, or chanting about her grace, all of which would be fitting. Rather, in this scene, as remembered in the antiphon of Vespers for the Assumption, the angels are requesting her fortitude.

This brings us back to the fortress of Santa Chiara. Saint Clare is often depicted holding an *ostensorium*, more commonly called a monstrance. In this lantern-like receptacle holding the Body of Christ, Saint Clare went out to the buttress wall and faced down the advancing Saracen soldiers. Miraculously, they were turned away.

What did she do? Two things: 1) she clung to her Savior and, 2) she was immobile, staring them down. Did it mean that Clare was without fear? Did it mean that she was audaciously daring? No. It means that she exercised the virtue of fortitude. Like the word *fortress*, from which it comes, fortitude is that virtue that was enjoined upon me by the daughter of St. Clare, that aged nun some 777 years after her spiritual mother St. Clare stood against the Saracens, as if to say, "The door is shut. You may not enter." She clung to the Word of God, literally, and stood her ground. Where did that strength come from? Confirmation.

Fortitude, as Joseph Pieper once wrote, presupposes vulnerability. One who cannot bleed need not fortify. What use is there for armor when your flesh is impenetrable? But we are vulnerable. We do bleed. Thus, the ultimate expression and essence of Christian fortitude is martyrdom. We naturally fear the loss of goods, and the greater the good the greater the fear. Life is the greatest good that we naturally possess and thus we naturally fear above all its loss. In other words, there is an order to fear, an *ordo timoris*. Christian fortitude, however, rises to such a power rooted in love for God that it is willing to forsake all things rather than lose that love. "He who fears the Lord will not be timid" (Sir 34:14).

There was an angel who once came to St. Joseph and commanded him not to fear to take Mary as his wife. We will always have fears in this life. We cannot vanquish them completely. Yet they can be ordered. They must be ordered by a holy fear. In some sense we can say that St. Joseph manifested his ordered fear in the fifth joyful mystery. He feared only one thing ultimately, the loss of the child, which in that case was the loss of God. All fear is subordinated to the fear of losing God.

Fortitude is most often associated with attack. It's true that often this virtue summons up the passion of anger and, if it remains virtuous, puts order back into an injustice by means of attack. Attack and endurance, says St. Thomas, are both possible actions flowing from the principle of fortitude. It is endurance, however, which the Angelic Doctor states is of the essence of fortitude. When one attacks, there is the possibility of victory. It is aided by anger, a proper response to an injustice. Endurance comes to the ready when there is nothing left to do but resist; nothing left to accomplish but stand strong and cling to the good.

This is the image of St. Clare, who clinging tightly to the greatest good, God himself literally in that *ostensorium*, stood like a tower of strength. She did not love her life so much that she lost it, but rather loved his life so dearly that she clung to it. For whom did she do this? For her daughters. No doubt many of her daughters inside the walls of the monastery were filled with fear and marveled at the fortitude of their Mother. St. Clare confirmed them. She gave them strength. That strength was not simply her own but rather from the fruition of the sacrament in her.

Character and Fruitfulness of the Sacrament

Sacramental character, as we have seen, configures us to divine worship. Baptismal character disposes us to actively receive the heavenly gifts from the Sacred Liturgy. Confirmation, in turn, strengthens us to cling to Christ's Eucharistic life despite fear, calumny, and ridicule. We are given the capacity not only to receive him but also to unite our sufferings with his passion, as true participants at the foot of the cross.

Thus do we return to the Tower of David and sing our praise to the *Stabat Mater*. This song that we traditionally sing as Catholics during the Stations of the Cross speaks of the woman who was standing at the cross in fortitude. She was a tower at the foot of the cross. Together they endured. The son of David, stretched out above that tower, conquered the Goliath of Satan not with an attack of five stones but with the five wounds of his enduring charity (the five wounds being his stigmata, the four in his feet and hands from the nails and the one in his side from the lance). He would not come down until his fortitude brought his act of obedient love to consummation.

And what of her, the tower who stood during it all? Why didn't she drag him down? Why not draw to herself that fruit of her womb from the tree of the cross? Her mother, Eve, was a woman promised death if she disobeyed and ate forbidden fruit. Eve grasped at equality with God in grasping the fruit. This woman, Mary, the new Eve, faced the death of Life himself. She had heard the word of God. She had harbored the Word of God. She had kept the Word of God. She stood as the sword Simeon spoke of pierced her through so that the thoughts of many hearts might be revealed (see Lk 2:34–35). She did not swoon. She stood. She suffered. Yet she did not take him down. On the contrary, she participated in the Passion with her compassion (meaning "to suffer with"). We can rightly say that she assisted him to die.

The result? Triumph! The fruition? See how in the book of Revelation St. John, who was there and saw her at the cross, overlays his words onto the passage from the Song of Songs that we examined: "And a great portent appeared in heaven, a woman clothed with the sun, with the moon under her feet, and on her head a crown of twelve stars" (Rv 12:1).

Who is she that comes forth like that dawn? The woman. She who precedes the sun with the first hint of light. Beautiful as the moon? The moon which gives witness to us through the night that the sun has not left us. The moon witnesses to the sun's return. This moon is her footstool. She is not simply as beautiful as the moon. The moon's beauty serves her. Finally, she is not simply brilliant as the sun but rather she is clothed with it, like a mantle. More than the gold gilding adorning the perishable wood of the arc, she is clothed with the brilliance of the sun. Glorious things are said of you O city of God! And that army? Those stars of the heavenly host make of themselves a living crown, dancing around their Queen. This is the fruit of her fortitude. As a perfect image of her Son, she too has been clothed with power and stands in loving witness to him. This is what we are configured to do by the first two sacraments of initiation, to participate in the Passion and receive the fruits of it.

CHAPTER 4

SACRAMENT OF DIVINE LIFE IN LOVE: HOLY EUCHARIST

CLINGING TO CHRIST

The Father's only-begotten Son, the desire of the everlasting hills (Gn 49:26), has come in the flesh. Those to whom he came, who had received the Father's Word in the flesh, could not bear to be without him. After three years of an itinerant life, the Apostles knew him as their life. Nevertheless, Christ told his disciples that there would come a time in which they would look for him but they would not find him (see Jn 7:34). The night before he died, Christ tenderly acknowledged their sorrow at his departure: "Truly, truly, I say to you, you will weep and lament, but the world will rejoice; you will be sorrowful, but your sorrow will turn into joy. When a woman is in travail she has sorrow, because her hour has come; but when she is delivered of the child, she no longer remembers the anguish, for joy that a child is born into the world. So you have sorrow now, but I will see you again and your hearts will rejoice, and no one will take your joy from you" (Jn 16:20–22).

More hearts than those of the Apostles would rejoice in Christ's return, for others were crushed with sorrow at his death. Mary Magdalene is an image of the Church as penitent and passionately in pursuit of him. What else did Mary have but Christ? Apart from him she wanted nothing on earth (Ps 72:25). The joy of his company had turned to sorrow unimaginable by his death. The words of the Song of Songs had become incarnate in her as she waited for the dawn to anoint Christ's body: "Upon my bed by night / I sought him whom my soul loves; / I sought him, but found him not; / I called him, but he gave no answer (Sg 3:1).

A sleepless night of echoing pain drove her out to find his body, to be near that which at least had been him, and to offer to that body an act of anointing love vivified by the memory of their first encounter. Christ told her to keep the ointment she possessed for the day of his burial, knowing full well she would not be allowed to anoint him. The Sabbath had precluded it. Was he setting up an appointment unknown to her in which he would manifest himself to her as resurrected? Even Christ rested on the Sabbath in the sleep of death. In the new day of recreation, he rose, and with this rising, hope was enkindled.

Magdalen's intense love for Christ did not allow her to wait for the dawn. This is a woman in whom no other desire had stirred, for whom no other object drew. Who would roll the stone away? Questions of practicality were not asked, for love hopes all things (1 Cor 13:7). She went, driven by desire for the absent one, and the only point of reference, the only locus she had, was a sacred body that was once his.[13]

She arrived but he was gone. How crushing this final blow must have been. Even when Peter and John had left the tomb to which she brought them, she remained transfixed. When the object of all one's love is not found, mobility is impossible because it is purposeless. There was nothing left for her to hope for. She weeps, for eyes that sought our Lord and found him not were now free to release the locks of bitter tears.[14] Her immobility, however, is shaken by the absence of the body. She was drawn to the body as a bittersweet attachment, as that which once belonged to the one she loved. Where had they laid him? She begins the search. What had she planned to do with the body if she had indeed found it? No doubt, as St. Thomas commented marveling at her undaunted and implacable resolution, she would have carried the body off with her if she could only find it. The body was the locus of the Word. The body was the presence of the One she lived for.

Then a voice called out. "Whom do you seek?"

The presence of what she thought to be a gardener moved Magdalene from sorrow to interrogation, seeking to assuage her longing. St. Thomas says that her eyes never met his. She questions him while her eyes sweep the terrain for some trace of the one she carried in her heart.[15] Her question to the gardener—who she would soon find out was no gardener at all—makes no mention of the one for whom she is looking.

---

[13] Christ's death entailed the separation of soul and body, but his body was not separated from his Godhead, according to St. Thomas. Cf. III q. 50 a. 4 ad 1.

[14] This image is taken from Augustine. Cf. *Catena in Jn.* c. 20 lec. 1.

[15] St. Thomas Aquinas, *Commentary on John's Gospel*, no. 251.

The nature of love is such that it becomes unimaginable to the lover that the object of this love could ever be unknown (cf. Sg 3:3). But the gardener does not answer her; he only pronounces her name. *Mary.* At hearing her name uttered by the one she loved, her Lord and Savior, she suddenly sees him and clings to him.

Such clinging, however, was futile. She was not permitted to arrest those feet from walking. He must ascend to his Father. She cannot hold him bound to her. Was she to lose again so swiftly, him whom she had found so recently? Was she to be bereft again of his physical presence, the joy and security of his voice? St. Paul said that once we knew Christ according to the flesh, but we know him in that way no longer (2 Cor 5:16). The Church, the Bride of Christ, would cling to him in a new way. She would seek his Body, be formed from his Body, adore his Body, build glorious cathedrals around his Body, compose polyphonic poems to sing about the gift of his Body.

Mary Magdalene was being instructed to move from Christ's body in the manner she had known it to his Eucharistic Presence which he gave to us. The sacrament of the Holy Eucharist would not be a diminishment of union but the only means of its true accomplishment. There is no need to feverishly cling to his feet to avoid separation, for the union which would be affected is stronger than her hands. Indeed, it is stronger than death. The profound joy, which this union of grace and charity will affect, shall never again be taken from her (Jn 16:22). So just what is the Holy Eucharist?

THE BODY AND BLOOD OF CHRIST

Christ's promise of returning to his disciples was not limited to the post-resurrection appearances, but also a return in his Spirit and in the sacraments. What do we want from our friends? We desire to be in their company, to be with them, to enjoy them. Christ does not leave us orphans. He sends us his Spirit and gives us his true Body and Blood.

Yet, as noted with Mary Magdalene, this presence is not the same. My senses do not perceive it. I cannot see him if I strain my eyes looking into the host. I am not pretending to see blood when the wine employed at Mass is red.

What is the Holy Eucharist? If it is only a symbol, Flannery O'Connor once quipped, "well then to hell with it." Far from being profane, this is perfectly precise. If it is bread, I and everyone else have been fools, believing a ridiculous lie. I should no more genuflect before the host than I should the bread in my cupboard.

But if it is what Christ said it is, then the only proper response is adoration. There is no adequate response that lies between these two poles. The only thing one cannot do when confronted with the reality of the Holy Eucharist is to be indifferent. If it is God's body, worship. If it is not, condemn it. Yet it is clear that while we desire to have those we love with us, it is nevertheless a fact that if this is his Body and Blood, our senses are given no access. I do not see him. I do not hear him. I cannot embrace him.

When someone dies, what consolation is there? We are often told that the deceased live in our hearts. Is that true? If my intentional memory is required, then it is I who am generating them. I can forget them or not think of them in a given moment. Do they therefore not exist? Either they exist or they do not. My memory of someone has nothing to do with his or her existence. I don't want a relationship with a memory. What any of us want is the presence of the beloved in all of their reality. We want them to confront us, to look at us, to react to us. In short, we want their bodily presence. This is the very thing Christ seemingly has denied to his friends. St. Thomas once said that when Christ walked among us, his divinity was concealed. Now when we look at the Sacred Host in adoration or Holy Mass, both his divinity *and* his humanity are hidden. Yet he is truth. Truth himself speaks truly, or there is nothing true. Why did he give himself to us in this manner?

In the sixth chapter of John, when Christ first mentions the gift of his Body and Blood, he allows for no confusion. "Unless you eat the flesh of the Son of man and drink his blood, you have no life in you. . . . My flesh is real food indeed and my blood drink indeed" (Jn 6:53, 55). When those around him balk at this in exasperation of the crudity, he only becomes more graphic by employing a word which means "to gnaw." He left no room for metaphor. He meant what he said. What he did not tell them was the means by which he would accomplish this. The Apostles, as noted above, remained with him because they know that he spoke the truth. He had the words of eternal life. They kept his word despite not yet understanding. They believed. For the present, he spoke no more of it.

But the subject returned on the night before he died. Christ was about to answer the question given by the angry crowd in John 6: "How can this man give us his flesh to eat?" Christ's life is not taken before it is first given. Christ gives himself to the Apostles in the upper room *before* the Passion takes place. He holds bread in his hand and tells them that it is his body. He tells them to take it. He tells them to eat it. The same is repeated with the chalice of wine, adding that this is his blood which will be poured out for the forgiveness of sins.

In this offering, he gives freely what will soon be taken; that is to say, his body and blood. Christ had told them that no one takes his life from him. He lays it down freely. Here, Christ commands that his disciples *take* his body and his blood (Mt 26:26). Divine wisdom and irony is at play once again. Christ's power and freedom to give himself makes the bloody act of taking his life on the cross, unknowingly, an act of obedience. In other words, he had already given up his body and commanded it to be taken in the upper room. The disciples fulfill this by reception. Those who took Christ in the Passion also fulfill this command. Christ's prior gift, in some sense, renders the violence of the Passion an act of obedience (cf. Jn 19:6, 18).

Christ's mode of giving himself is suited to our mode of reception. You and I cannot perceive spiritual realities. We receive gifts by means of sensible realities. We know the spiritual through the sensible. Furthermore, the effect of original sin in us causes us to live so much in the exterior life and so little in the interior. Christ came to redeem the whole person. In some sense, the mode of giving himself to us is remedial, in that we must make an interior act of faith, keep his word, and we will receive all that he has to give us even though our senses will not be able in this life (outside of extraordinary graces and miracles) to perceive what he is giving us.

As seen previously, Christ often employs material objects when working miracles, just as he uses his own flesh as an instrument of his divinity. In the miracle that prefaced Christ's first words on the Holy Eucharist, five barley loaves were employed. The Church Fathers contend that this has a spiritual meaning. Just as our five senses were absorbed in the material world, Christ would use that material world to draw us into the spiritual world and into his life. When we eat bread, we assimilate it into our body. When we eat *this* bread, we are assimilated into the Mystical Body.

Christ had said that God is spirit and the flesh itself is of no avail. However, Christ's flesh has Divine power and is life-giving in virtue of being God. This is a life which does not perish but endures unto eternal life. The Shepherd feeds his flock with his own body and blood.

It's not surprising that this "hard saying" was neither understood nor received. In every age, each person must cooperate with grace or refuse it when confronted with this sublime teaching. Is it truly him? He did not intend for us to consume his Body in the manner in which we eat the flesh of animals. The flesh of itself as he said is of no avail. To receive the Holy Eucharist under the appearances of bread and wine is an act of faith and love, since it is not bread and wine we are receiving but the true Body and Blood of Christ. Eating human flesh is cannibalism. Eating nothing but flesh is worthless. But to receive his Body and Blood, their substance under the sensible qualities of bread and wine? To have true communion with him? This is life and life eternal! Our Lord thus gives us that which feeds the interior man, forming a union unparalleled in nature. In the other sacraments, Christ is operative. In this sacrament, Christ *is* there substantially and bodily. What we all long for is genuine communion (union) of substance. Bodies do not create true union. They have borders.

Christ gives himself to us in such a fashion that the contact is like any bread or wine, while the reality is Christ's bodily substance.

SACRIFICE OF THE MASS

The Holy Mass is called a sacrifice not because Christ is crucified again. Rather, it is called this because you and I participate in his one and eternal sacrifice "re-presented" (made present again) to us in an unbloody manner. The sacrifice of the cross and the sacrifice of the Mass are numerically one, present in different modalities.

This should not be surprising. The Lord, as seen previously, offered himself *before* the events of the bloody crucifixion. In other words, the Last Supper was the same sacrifice as that which we offer, which in turn is the same sacrifice of the cross. *There is no new sacrifice in the Holy Eucharist but a different mode of the same sacrifice.* Holy Mass is not a mere recollection but rather a re-presentation of the Passion. We now participate by acts of loving devotion in that which we previously only participated in by sinfulness. In other words, our sins were present at the cross. So too by the power of the Mass are our acts of sacrificial love. The one eternal offering is applied to diverse times and places in fulfillment of his command to "do this." The Passion was willed by the Savior as oblative love. This act of his now quickens our own will to imitate the "desire" of our Lord (Lk 22:15). In some sense, we can say that what he willed *then* infuses our will *now* to do what he does; through this imitation, we offer ourselves to the Father in him. He is offered and we are offered in him.

One of the ways this is sacramentally represented is

through the double consecration. Following the example and commandment of Christ at the Last Supper, first bread is consecrated and then the wine. Why? What is the cause of his death on the cross but the separation of his Body from his Blood? Christ is not offered again, but sacramentally this is manifested by the separate consecrations. Similarly, the Resurrection is sacramentally manifested. You may have noticed that after the Our Father, the priest places a small particle of the Host into the chalice. This reunification is a sign of the Resurrection, and for this reason, the priest can speak the words of Christ to you that were spoken to his Apostles after his resurrection: "Peace be with you."

ELEMENTS OF THE SACRAMENT

Along with Baptism, the matter, form, and minister of this sacrament have been explicitly dictated by Christ himself. He took bread. He took wine. He commanded the Apostles to "do this." But why bread and wine?

The antecedents in the Old Testament are plenty, not least of which is the offering made by that mysterious priest Melchizedek (see Gn 14). In one sense, bread is the simplest staple of human life, while wine has about it a certain nobility. Both are worked on by human intelligence, giving to natural objects a further perfection. Wheat becomes bread. Grapes become wine. One thing is given as a fact of nature, and when directed by intelligence, it becomes something more. When our Lord fed the five thousand, he did not create bread from nothing, but from bread, he multiplied. When he preformed his first miracle at the Wedding Feast of Cana, he did not simply place wine in the stone water jars. Rather, he first had them filled with water which he would then change into superior wine. Perhaps part of the answer is found in the cooperative nature of the sacrament. We make something to be more than it would be left unto itself. He makes from that infinitely more than it could hope to be left unto itself, namely, his Body and Blood. Furthermore, by our consuming his sacred body, he makes us into his Mystical Body. In other words, we normally assimilate food to ourselves, but in the Eucharist, we are assimilated to Christ and are "knit up" into his body, the Church.

The effect of these sacramental elements is twofold: nourishment and joy. Man does not live on bread alone; he needs the joy that comes from genuine love. The Most Holy Eucharist in its *sacramentum,* or sign, speaks to these two realities. It nourishes the divine life in us as bread sustains the body and we are given the spiritual joy of sober inebriation. As wine "cheers man's heart," so too do we, by this communion, experience the joy that is the fruit of his love. Just as the material sign points to the grace to be received, the words, as we noted, direct that matter to a higher end. In this case, Christ's words, having the power of creation, designate the substance of bread and the substance of wine to become his Body and Blood.

In this most sublime sacrament, the *vis fluens*, the flowing power, does not pass through the elements as with water. The Eucharist is not an instrument of giving grace. Christ is not simply active in this sacrament, this sacrament *is* Christ. In his wisdom, Christ ordained certain men to be the instruments themselves by which this would happen. The priest, as the Church teaches, acts in the very person of Christ. This is the reason the priest wears sacred vesture. He no longer acts simply as an individual man with all of his particular characteristics. He loses himself in Christ. Christ employs his hands. The priest gives over his tongue, speaking in the first person, in the person of Christ. Christ offers himself in and through the priest. It is a personal act, and Christ employs a person to accomplish it.

EFFECTS OF THE SACRAMENT

With respect to the effects of the Holy Eucharist, we must look on the subject in the same way we discern the effects of the Incarnation itself. Christ Incarnate is the same whether by the shores of Galilee or contained under the sacramental species. The difference, aside from the mode by which he is contained, is that which the sacrament signifies. This signification will also determine the nature of the effects. He who came into the world visibly, bestowing life and grace, is the same one who, under a visible species of bread and wine, bestows upon us who receive him that life and grace. The spiritual nourishment and the joyful inebriation that the species suggests progressively invade our souls the more we cling to the Eucharist.

Remember that the life-giving Word of God, by uniting himself to his own flesh, made his flesh vivifying. Therefore, it was fitting for him in a certain way to be united to our bodies through his sacred flesh and precious blood. The life we received in Baptism and the strengthening of Confirmation require nourishment. The character of both of those sacraments makes possible and makes us eager for the consummation of Holy Communion.

St. John's Gospel is replete with examples where contact

with Christ's flesh had a vivifying effect upon the recipient. His flesh objectively carried such vivifying power, but the subject who received the effect of such power had also to be disposed to receive it. The woman who touched his tassel and the man who received his sight (Jn 9:6) were those who united faith to the active power of Christ's flesh. Bodily proximity or even reception, as will be shown further, is not sufficient to receive the effects that flow from Christ's body. As with any food, we have to be able to receive and assimilate this food. If the spiritual food, the Eucharistic bread and spiritual drink, find in our souls a ready disposition, they cause divine life to grow in us and yield in the soul not nourishment alone but spiritual delight.

In addition to nourishment, we are ushered into active participation of the passion of Christ. Have you ever read the accounts of Christ's passion in the Gospels, stared at a crucifix, prayed the Stations of the Cross, and longed to be able to make a response to so great an act of love? We are not only spectators in the Passion. By virtue of the Mass, *we are participants in it*, not by bodily activism, but by internal offering. We are to approach the Mass, in the words of St. John Chrysostom, as if to drink from Christ's own side from which blood is poured out for the remission of sins. The Holy Eucharist is a sacrament and a sacrifice and thus benefits in these two ways, being offered to all who partake of it. The offering of Christ is acceptable and pleasing to the Father as a perfect act of obediential love. What we are attempting to do is unite our offerings with his and pray that they are acceptable.

We do this not only for ourselves but for the whole Body of Christ. Other sacraments, St. Thomas argues, benefit only the recipient. The Holy Eucharist, being both a sacrament and a sacrifice, thus benefits all those who are dying with Christ. Christ's passion, on the one hand, benefits all, for in his great love, he died for his enemies, that they might become friends. Nevertheless, the effect of the Passion is not attained except by those who are united to the Passion by faith and charity. So too the Eucharistic sacrifice, which is the re-presentation of the one eternal sacrifice, has no effect except upon those who are united to the sacrament by faith and charity.

Thomas concludes by noting that *receiving* belongs to the nature of the sacrament, but *offering* belongs to the nature of sacrifice. To receive, therefore, benefits those who actually receive the sacrament. To receive one, two, or more hosts cannot increase the effect of the sacrament since the one Christ is contained under one or many. However, the oblation of the sacrifice is multiplied in several Masses, and in that sense, the effect of the sacrifice and of the sacrament is multiplied (the latter, presumably, because there are thus more recipients).

This sacrificial banquet and its effects are for those who are Christ's friends, who have been redeemed by his sacrifice and to whom he commits the effects of his passion. He does this by offering to them his very Body and Blood. We participate now in the wedding banquet, the heavenly banquet, by way of this sacrament. Human nature, St. Thomas states, was espoused to the Divine nature in the wedding chamber of the womb of the Virgin. Individual souls are wedded to God by faith, and when the feast is prepared, the servants, who are also friends being espoused, come to banquet. "Everything is ready; come to the marriage feast" (Mt 22:4)!

Finally, the species under which Christ's Body and Blood appear as bread and wine signifies unity, just as bread comes from the harvest of many grains and wine from many grapes.

The reception of this sacrament has the effect, as seen previously, of changing us into that which is eaten, instead of what is eaten being transformed into the consumer. The love of Christ transforms the one who feeds on his Body and Blood into an active lover of Christ.

What does active mean? I wish to emphasize the way in which the sacrament urges us toward the acts of friendship with Christ. The love of Christ received in his Body and Blood urges us to reciprocal acts of love (see 2 Cor 5:14). The union created in Christ's love is the distinguishing mark of the Church, as all the members are incorporated by Christ's charity into one body. Unity is the *raison d'être* of the sacrament. Christ suffered his passion in charity in order that he might unite to himself his spouse, namely, the Church (cf. Eph 5).

Union and delectation, as in friendship, reveal themselves to be two aspects of the same reality. This increase of charity increases union and, consequently, delight in the one given to us in the sacrament. This union of Head and members and their mutual delight will be fulfilled in heaven but is begun here and participated in now. In heaven, glory will consist in two things that will most delight us, namely, the enjoyment of God and of the society of the communion of saints, our friends. There is no delight in possessing a good without someone to share it with. Any good experienced causes a movement in us to share, even if only by recounting with the ones we love such that they, too, might share in our joy. It is true that the possession of God is our ultimate good, leaving nothing to be desired. Yet just as God is fullness himself but delights in us, so too can we become full in God and yet also be able to delight in God's friends. We were made to feed on love, but if that love is not infinite, it leaves us hungry.

Ravenously must we devour when infinite love is not our feast, for we will never be satisfied by the finite. When he is our all, however, we will also delight in the love of all in the Mystical Body.

In summary, the signification of the sacrament points to nourishment, delight, and sacrifice. The reality that comes about by Christ's action is the actual transubstantiation of simple bread and wine into his true Body and true Blood. The ultimate effect of this sacrament is the unity of the Body of Christ, the Church in charity.

But what if the recipient does not love? How many times have we seen someone (often ourselves) come straight from Mass with the same wicked behavior that preceded it? Did that person (we) receive the actual Body and Blood of Christ? What if the priest himself was wicked before and after? Did he truly confect the Body and Blood of Christ? Neither the priest's piety nor the fidelity of the recipient changes the objectivity of the Body and Blood. For our participation and reception to be fruitful, we must possess active faith and charity to receive. Let us turn now to fruitful participation and reception of this sacrament.

FRUITFULNESS OF THE SACRAMENT

Bread, wine, form, and priest. These four elements are essential. The Church has historically woven a tapestry of beauty around these humble realties to assist the faithful to *see* what is taking place and to assist in the offering. The "rites" of the Church are the various ways in which the Sacrifice of the Mass is offered. The Church employs gestures, vestments, chant, incense, and all the sublime art and architecture inspired by love of this sacrament.

The patrimony of the Church is not pointless pomp. There are things worthy of celebration. There are realities so sublime and so delicate to demand veils of layered meaning. Every rite is clothed with material majesty to manifest the spiritual reality. To expose those rites to capricious stripping is to attempt to shame them. Attempts at making the rites relevant or mundane is an attempt to make man the measure of the divine action. I will never comprehend his action. I shall never reduce transubstantiation to the measure of my mind. By making everything "understandable," I have in effect made the action more incomprehensible. *I state with the ordinary that there is nothing extraordinary.* In short, I have lied. While the glorious ceremonies of the Church never attain to the glory of God as it truly is, the unveiling has revealed less, not more. External beauty requires external sacrifice. In addition to this, internal sacrifice is required.

The fruitfulness of this sacrament demands a certain reciprocity. Is there anything more beautiful than his act of oblative love? I must respond in kind. I must make an interior offering of self to accompany my bodily offering of gesture, song, and beauty as the response to his sublime act. What man among you would find it pleasing to have at once sacrificed something great for the woman you love, only to have her respond with indifference? If you came home from battle having fought through death and returned beyond all hope, what would you expect to see on the face of your beloved? Presumably surprise and ecstatic joy that bursts forth in song, celebration, and pageantry. Our love for "keeping it simple" is often a sign of our lack of love for the One who returns. I am not using this metaphor to be dramatic. It is fully dramatic. It is the divine comedy.

Our Lord often spoke of a King who returns from a long absence. What will he find when he returns, Christ often asked. In some sense, every Mass is a dress rehearsal. He comes to us truly, but now in a form that does not impress upon our senses. We are able to make acts of faith. We are to act from love's volition, not from obligation. Our longing takes the form of preparation, of engagement, and of resting in his advent. If we come to the Mass without such love for him, we should beg for it. We can receive him sacramentally in Holy Communion without sanctification. It is the faith and desire of the woman that drew forth from Christ healing at the touching of his tassel. We draw by longing. We draw by love. How much more we could draw, we who touch not a tassel but consume his very Body!

Another analogy Christ used to speak about his coming was that of a wedding feast. Recall that on one occasion a man was asked to come, seemingly after others had refused. This man was nevertheless censured for not having on a wedding garment. The reaction of the Father of the bridegroom seems severe. "But when the king came in to look at the guests, he saw there a man who had no wedding garment; and he said to him, 'Friend, how did you get in here without a wedding garment?' And he was speechless. Then the king said to the attendants, 'Bind him hand and foot, and cast him into the outer darkness; there men will weep and gnash their teeth'" (Mt 22:11–14).

Why such a reaction? The King begins by calling the man "friend." To be there was to be clothed in the friendship of his son; it is to be clothed with divine charity (Rom 13:14).

Not only can we manifest a lack of love by refusing to come as so many did in this parable, we can also come without the baptismal garment of divine love.

Furthermore, if we receive him in Holy Communion without reconciling with him first, we commit sacrilege. Why so harsh? Imagine infidelity in a marriage. Can such infidelity readily admit a return to marital intimacy? Marriage in some sense is the greatest of friendships. In marriage, the intimacy of one's bodily life is given to the other because of a prior donation of the interior life by the vows exchanged. The vows are then "made flesh." This consummation of a prior intention renders the sacrament indissoluble. The "one flesh union" of marriage is an image of the Incarnation itself. Words are exchanged and life (potentially) is procreated.

The sacrament of marriage is a sign itself of a greater reality, namely, Christ's marriage to his bride, the Church. The analogy and fulfillment of the "one flesh union" signified by marriage and fulfilled in the Holy Eucharist can and has been made. However, despite the most honest efforts of a married couple, carnal knowledge, domestic association, the communication of one's mind, the concord of their respective wills, and the consolation and joy which comes in virtue (and sacrament) of their marital friendship, their marriage is an image of the reality, not the reality itself.

That which "brings together" a man and a woman also divides. One can get only so close before hitting the barrier of the other. To ask of flesh more than it can provide is a lesson in futility. In other words, one receives or contacts a body when interior communion is desired. The body is not rendered unimportant, as it is an essential part of the other. But the body alone is insufficient. What I wish to suggest is that Christ gives us in the sacrament, not himself as sensible, but rather himself as substantial, a union of substances. This is Holy Communion, but it is dependent upon an interior disposition of self-offering. We must receive Holy Communion spiritually as well as sacramentally, otherwise the latter is of no avail. Sacraments are not magic.

Take, for example, the way in which the Blessed Virgin and the beloved disciple participated in the Passion itself. There were soldiers. There were bystanders. There were those who hated Christ and those few who loved him. All had the same relative physical proximity, but Our Lady who stood there offering him and offering herself participated differently. John and Magdalen, who offered themselves by faith and charity, were quite different from the participation of the soldiers or priests. One thief marvelously gained eternal life by a simple request prompted by faith, while the other received not a word. All of the Apostles, according to St. Thomas, received the most Holy Eucharist from the hands of the Savior himself, but the effects were quite different.

Love provokes in us a desire to receive the One we love, while filial fear gives rise to reverential humility. We who approach to receive should have first offered in the context of the Mass our sacrifice of praise. If we are devoutly longing, let us receive; if we have not offered and have not devotion, let us wait and pray for our hunger to grow.

Let us invoke the saints who unambiguously and unanimously pledged their lives for the sacrament of the altar. St. Catherine of Siena, before she had received permission to receive the Holy Eucharist every day, had been denied one day by a priest. No doubt the priest feared that, by receiving too often, she might grow too accustomed to this marvelous wonder. While she was in the back of the massive nave of San Domenico in Siena, as the priest went to reunite the Body and Blood at the fraction rite of the Mass, the particle, instead of falling into the Precious Blood in the chalice, sailed through the air to the back of the basilica where the saint received it reverently into her mouth.

After Mass, the priest asked St. Catherine what happened. She replied simply: "I asked you and you refused. I asked my Beloved and he said yes." Let us pray for this fervent desire!

Before he died, the great Doctor of the Holy Eucharist, St. Thomas Aquinas, spoke these words after he received the sacrament for the last time:

> I have received you, price of my soul's redemption, I receive you, viaticum of my pilgrimage, for love of whom I have studied, watched, labored; I have preached you, I have taught you; never have I said any-thing against you, and if I have done so it is through ignorance and I do not grow stubborn in my error; if I have taught ill on this sacrament or others, I submit it to the judgment of the Holy Roman Church, in obedience to which I leave now this life.[16]

This is the perfect response to the gift of himself in the Eucharist. St. John of the Cross says we will be judged on our death bed by how we have loved. Christ did not spare himself. All was given. All is required in the marvelous exchange of divine friendship.

---

[16] Translation, Torrell, vol. 1, 293.

CHAPTER 5

SACRAMENT OF DIVINE LOVE LIVED: MARRIAGE

IN THE BEGINNING

It seems fitting to discuss sacramental marriage at this juncture since it is an image of what takes place in the one flesh union of the Holy Eucharist. I highlight *sacramental* marriage because this union is first a natural reality before it becomes a supernatural one. The Church, in her blessing of the couple at the wedding ceremony, states that marriage is one of the gifts that was not washed away with the Flood. It remained a natural sign of something for which we could not have hoped, namely, God's marriage with his people.

What did God intend marriage to be? Confusion swirls around this natural institution now more than ever. Confusion obscures the natural, but from where does this confusion come? We do not normally have confusion about other natural realities. No one is proclaiming that we should no longer sleep, eat, or drink. No one decries that those activities were part of an ignorant past and we, the enlightened of the present, have no further use of such outmoded conventions. Sex has nothing to do with gender, and gender has nothing to do with sex. Gender now has nothing even to do with biology. Why all this confusion?

The answer is simple. Sin. It is an unpopular answer. Yet what happens with sin is confusion. The mind is darkened and we cannot see things for what they are. We distort reality, seeing the world through warped glass. Part of the Good News that the Gospel brings is the truth about the human person. This truth is that God has made the human person male and female as a revelation of himself. Only Christ can perfectly reveal man to himself since only Christ was perfect man without distortion.

When Christ is questioned about the liceity of divorce (Mt 19), he states clearly that in the beginning it was not so. Only in the Word through whom all things were made can we read what it is to be male and female. How did he design us? When I say designed, I am not referring to mechanical parts. I mean purpose. When one finds an artifact and doesn't know its purpose, the clearest and quickest answer is to ask the designer. How did he make us, to what end, for what purpose? Christ's use of the words "in the beginning" bring us back to Genesis. Only Christ as the "new Adam" can walk across the bridge of time and give us a glimpse into the Creator's beautiful handiwork before it was distorted by sin. What do we see when we look at "the beginning?"

Unlike other accounts of the world's beginning, Genesis is marked with the tranquility of God's sovereignty. He creates neither out of necessity nor out of strife. He speaks creation into existence through his word. Each time he creates, he seems to rest in the contemplation of his work by pronouncing it good. Goodness is that which is desirable. Goodness is that which achieves the end for which it was made. All things, insofar as they exist, are good. Evil, which classically is defined as an absence of good that should be present, has not entered into history at this point. This is a startling fact if you take a moment to consider it. Evil is all around us, both moral and physical. The temptation historically with moral evil is to find it in things, structures, and externals, not in the heart of man.

When I was a newly ordained priest, I was tasked by my brothers to pick up some supplies for a birthday party. Others were handling the main part of the meal, but my task was essential: chocolate cake and beer. I was in the checkout line, in a cassock no less, when I heard the "*tsk tsk*" of someone behind me. I turned and asked if I could help her. The southern gentlewoman said to me in a beautiful accent: "You should be ashamed of yourself. A man of the cloth. Chocolate cake and beer!" I smiled and asked her if she had ever read Genesis. She retorted that she had. I asked her what God had said when he created. I answered for her. "He said that it was good! And if they had had enough paper they would eventually have written down chocolate cake and beer." Creation is good. Our employment of it, on the other hand, can be quite evil.

Man, he proclaims, is very good. Why does he create them "male and female?" Clearly this was unnecessary. Why have these bodies that differentiate us? You cannot say it was solely for reproduction. Could he not have made us in such a way so as to allow for the propagation of the species in an asexual fashion? In some sense, no. If he desired us to be in his image and likeness, there is something about that image and likeness of which the complementarity of the sexes plays a part. Watch what happens in Genesis. In the second creation account, the man is created but it was not good for him to be alone. Why not?

If we are in the image and likeness of God, and God is a communion of persons, not solitude, we, too, are made for the purpose of communion. We want to know and to be known, to love and to be loved. It was not good for the man to be alone because of the image that was in him. It was not good for him to be alone because the Original is not alone. God is the Original; we are derivative. He is a communion of Persons, and thus we are made for communion. What is the solution? The animals are brought forth to the man, but not one was sufficient. He could know them but they could not know him. Never did he stare into the eyes of an aardvark and cry, "At last!" What is Genesis trying to teach? That nothing is man's equal. Nothing else shares in his life's breath, the divine breath, the capacity to know, to know that we know, to seek ends, to direct ourselves to those ends, to consider our actions. Man has an interior life, as we saw, that needs to be inhabited.

So God casts the man into a deep sleep. This sleep is a kind of death. We lose control when we sleep. It is in some sense a preparation for death. This gift of life, the life that man himself was given by God, would require a kind of death. God takes from him a rib. Why a rib? I have heard many interesting interpretations over the years. Some say it signifies woman standing at his side. Most women I have polled say it is close to the man's heart. Most men I have polled say he has many to spare (spare ribs). Whatever the case, it seems that the word *rib* is a play on the word *life*. This one who is to be built up must have what the man has. The man has something similar to the life of God: spirit. For this woman to be like the man, the gift of his life is required. From this "life" God will build up the woman. The man will in turn follow the path of the rib by giving his life precisely where the life was given: the woman. He follows the trail.

When God brings the woman to the man, we hear the first exclamation of joy in creation.[17] We can hear the burden of time and solitude in his voice. He was waiting. He was longing. He was to be a person in communion. The woman spoke not a word. Adam saw what she was. What revealed this to him was her body. There was no need of extensive research into equality of the sexes, nor a course on gender studies. Her body and his were complimentary. I do not mean to suggest that he saw *only* her body; it is after the Fall that they realized that they were naked. What this means, of course, is that there was innocence. This type of innocence is not that of children who have not the faculty of reason operative. This is not the shamelessness of adults who have forsaken innocence in a show of liberation and empowerment. Shamelessness is a sign that one's reason sees nothing worth protecting, sees nothing good worth treasuring as a gift to be given and not taken. The innocence of the first couple was one that comes from order.

Pope St. John Paul II called it the tranquility of the interior gaze. It is peace. They didn't need to be afraid or ashamed. There was literally nothing to hide. There was only the simple marveling in their existence, in the existence of the other. This, as Josef Pieper once noted, is the first movement of rational love, the statement exchanged by their gaze which said to the other: "It is good that you are here!" Adam didn't see a body, he saw the woman.

The first command Adam and Eve received was to be

---

[17]   The now popularized "Theology of the Body" of Pope St. John Paul II makes this point.

fruitful and multiply. Commandments were not always so burdensome to follow! Their very complementarity made the nuptial meaning of their bodies capable of self-donation, a kind of donation which would result in fruitfulness. How often we forget that the act of conjugal life involves more than two persons. We properly call it "procreation" as the couple participates in the creative activity of God. For life to be created, a soul created *ex nihilo* (Latin for "out of nothing") comes forth from God at the moment of conception. Imagine, if you will, that at some point when the conjugal act is finished, an hour, two hours, a day, the Lord and giver of life makes his donation to the act, and creates. Two in a room becomes three. The only One who knows that a new person exists is God, though the woman's body will soon tell her and she will soon tell her husband. How fitting for the three of them to unhesitatingly give praise to God who has visited them and made the land of their love fruitful.

As we saw in our discussion of the Holy Eucharist, this exquisite reality is also a sign of God's marriage to the individual soul, making each a member of his own Body, the Church. As a sign, Christ has raised the natural reality of marriage to the level of a sacrament. It now becomes a sign of Christ and his Church. Reciprocal self-donation began with the New Adam giving his life, his fullness of life, to us from the cross. His pierced side now flows to us who would receive him at the base of the cross, participating in self-donating love unto a consummate union. Making them "male and female" reaches into the highest level of sign. Female is a sign to the male: "Love here." Male is a sign to the female: "Love here." The idea of the gift is inscribed into our flesh. The body has a nuptial meaning in itself. Christ is man. The Church, in her turn, every soul, is spoken of mystically as feminine. Each soul must allow his death for us, admit his death for us, receive the fruit of his death for us. But this donation does not stop at the level of the gift. We are not barren fig trees. We are meant to receive, to gestate grace, and bring it forth in abundant fruit.

The goods of marriage are therefore easy to see. St. Augustine first articulated them when the heresy of Manicheanism was rife, attacking the goodness of creation and the beauty of children. He stated succinctly that the "goods" of marriage are the good of chaste fidelity, the good of children, and the good of an indissoluble bond.

The first good we can see is depicted in Genesis. Chastity restores man. It gives him the capacity to possess himself so as to make a sincere gift of himself. The unchaste man cannot make a sincere gift of self, much less to just one. Grace is needed for this. Christ has come to restore men and women to their nobility such that they will not even look upon another with lust. He goes down into man's heart where donation is warped into a gift to self and transforms it to a self-gift. He *unbends* man, coiled as he is on himself, locked in a self-embrace of futility, and opens him up for love of another.

The second good, that of children, demands conversion of heart. If the above takes place, the couple is then free to share their love. Love breaks the borders of both their individuality as well as their singular union. Goodness is diffusive of itself. If love is allowed to live and to grow, it necessarily overflows its banks in blessings. Love becomes incarnate in children, borne from the chaste and confident fidelity of the donation of spouses.

Finally, since the above requires combat and self-mastery, a bond is forged by God, the links of which no human tribunal can break. A vow, G. K. Chesterton once quipped, is not made for the moment in which it is taken. Rather, it is made for a moment in the future in which it will be needed. A young couple in love needs no such vow. It is needed precisely when love is pressed, when goods compete, when suffering comes. It is a glorious adventure not made by the faint of heart but by those willing to donate their lives. What seems to be restricting human freedom proves to be the opening of true freedom and adventure. The circumference of a wedding ring is narrow indeed, but once the finger is through, infinite possibilities open up and the hand clasps around another's as together they stare into a future of promise and Providence.

ELEMENTS OF THE SACRAMENT

Marriage is a natural institution created by God as a sign witnessing to himself as a God who is love. Raised to the level of a sacrament, it is employed to manifest God's love not only in himself but his donation in Christ to his Church. Though this donation is natural and ubiquitous, its ritual structure varies considerably from culture to culture. Nevertheless, as with all of the sacraments, there are elements which are essential.

First, what is the material sign of the sacrament? Is it the procession? The father of the bride brings his daughter to the bridegroom as an image of creation when God the Father brought the first woman to the first man. Even the most cynical in the arena of love stands and springs of hope are engendered in every heart at this moment. While the procession, as lovely as it is, is not necessary, two elements are: a man and a woman. Their very bodies, as we saw in our discussion of creation, have a nuptial meaning. They are capable of donation unto fruition. By this is not meant only conjugal life (which is essential for consummation and therefore indissolubility) but all that goes with a bodily life. Spiritual capacities are not defined by male and female, but their employment is conditioned by being male and female. Each sex has certain bodily capacities that compliment the other, all of which are helpful for the fruitfulness not simply of conception but nurturing and education of children. The data on this is indisputable.

Recall that as a sacrament, the Lord has elevated something natural to something that bestows grace. The sign tells us something about the grace being received. This signification of male and female manifests that the grace bestowed is going to effect self-donation in a way far beyond the capricious limitations of human volition. The vows which are taken speak to this further signification by designating the other as the *locus* of their donation. The couple is presented to each other before the priest as well as the Church. As marriage is a sign of Christ's union with his Church, it is thus that the Church is present. This is a public reciprocal donation and we are called to witness that it, in fact, happened.

The words declared can vary, but they must indicate that this donation is total, exclusive, faithful, and fruitful. These elements are the very goods described above by St. Augustine. The couple cannot withhold in word or intention these goods to the other in order for the sacrament to be valid. Similarly, the couple must each be free to do so and not under constraint or with impediments. The reason for this is demanded by what is exchanged. It is not a contract in which goods and services are rendered, but rather an exchange of persons in a covenantal relationship.

Once these vows are exchanged, the sacrament exists. The

couple is married. That said, the marriage is not yet indissoluble. Like the Incarnation itself in which Divinity was wed to humanity in the womb of the Virgin, so too the couple proceeds to the *thalamo*, the wedding chamber, in which the words they spoke become flesh in consummate union. Once consummated, this sacramental sign becomes indissoluble. Why? Because it is more than their volition. What *God* has joined not only may we not separate, we are unable to so do (Mt 19:6). It has been forged with divine bands.

EFFECTS OF THE SACRAMENT

What is effected is called the marriage bond. There is in the liturgy of Matrimony an *epiclesis* which means a calling down of the Holy Spirit. God *seals* the covenant. One of the expressions of this found historically in the Sacred Liturgy is curious. The priest would take the hands of the couple and wrap his stole around them, binding them as it were, not with their own strength but with the power of Christ (the stole of the priest represents Christ's priestly authority and power). This *bond* is not bondage. It is true freedom. When we do not bind ourselves to others we never experience conversion or the true joy of fidelity. Indeed the very word *religion* means to re-bind us to God, having been loosened from his love into the abyss of futility (*re-ligare*).

Christ does not complete his work in the couple by forging a bond and then walking away and leaving them to their own devices. When the wedding is over and the honeymoon is a distant memory, the grace of the sacrament sets to work. Its power, when cooperated with, perfects the couple's love and strengthens their indissoluble unity. It prepares and calls them to expand, to diffuse the goodness God has given to them into the fullness of a family.

How does the couple best cooperate? While the Church might seem to be naïve in her incessant optimism in regards to marriage, such sight is based not upon human capacity but upon the sacrament. We believe in divine power. We believe that Christ's love for his Church, like the vows spoken, is total, exclusive, faithful, and fruitful. This power is in the hands bound and "ringed" in the sacrament of Matrimony. Each marriage will have its own sufferings relative to the purifications necessary but also the unique way in which Christ has chosen this couple to participate in his passion. This and this alone will make it truly fruitful.

THE FRUITFULNESS OF THE SACRAMENT

Recall that all of the sacraments receive their power from the passion of Christ, lead to it, and find their fulfillment in it. I think we can see a paradigm for marital life in the liturgy of Matrimony. The wedding takes place in the context of the Sacrifice. It was once the case that the couple actually came into the sanctuary for the exchange of vows. The bridegroom leaves with his bride after the sacrifice. What does all this denote?

The couple, in some sense, is reenacting the Incarnation, Passion, Death and Resurrection of Christ. It is the Paschal Mystery that gives meaning and efficacy to their lives. First, they come in body and exchange words one to the other. They then participate in the Holy Mass. They are present there in the sanctuary. The final goal of the marriage is to reach the eternal marriage of heaven. But the man, as an image of Christ, can only escort the woman, herself an image of the Church, back to the Father because of their participation in the passion of Christ, the Mass. They have partaken of his redemptive act and have eaten the heavenly food of the one-flesh union.

What I mean to suggest is that the sacrament of Matrimony takes place within the space of an hour during Holy Mass. Yet what happens there will continue to unfold throughout the life of the couple. In the redemption of human love, the redemption of human life and family, Christ has given us a sacrament to go back *to the beginning* but *through* the passion of his cross. Our ever-failing attempt to return to Edenic bliss without the power of the cross is what makes us cynical in love. We are consistently disappointed. Our attempts are futile. Human love in its youth and vigor can indeed feel as if one has been transported to a new life, a new world, in which all things will be well so long as the other is with me. What happens when suffering comes? What happens when the other is not sufficient to assuage my anguish? Sufferings are inevitable. Making them redemptive is not. Here the grace of the sacrament is discharged for those who engage it.

In Ephesians chapter five, we read the following:

> Be subject to one another out of reverence for Christ. Wives, be subject to your husbands, as to the Lord. For the husband is the head of the wife as Christ is the head of the Church, his body, and is himself its Savior. As the Church is subject to Christ, so let wives also be subject in everything to their husbands. Husbands, love your wives, as Christ loved the Church and gave himself up for her, that he might sanctify her, having

cleansed her by the washing of water with the word, that he might present the Church to himself in splendor, without spot or wrinkle or any such thing, that she might be holy and without blemish. Even so husbands should love their wives as their own bodies. He who loves his wife loves himself. For no man ever hates his own flesh, but nourishes and cherishes it, as Christ does the Church, because we are members of his body. "For this reason a man shall leave his father and mother and be joined to his wife, and the two shall become one flesh." This is a great mystery, and I mean in reference to Christ and the Church; however, let each one of you love his wife as himself, and let the wife see that she respects her husband. (Eph 5:21–33)

This passage is what I like to call the elbow reading. When it is read at Holy Mass, usually the man gets an elbow or the woman does as a sort of "uh-huh!? You see?" Pastors tend to avoid speaking about this passage, relegating it to historical convention. Yet if the "great mystery" (*mystery* is the Greek word for sacrament) is this union of Christ and his Church, and if human marriage as a sacrament is a sign of this, we cannot forsake this passage if we want to understand the potency that is given to each couple with that exchange of vows. How do we interpret it?

First, mutual subjection is enjoined. You have given your lives away one to the other as ministers of this sacrament. You are subject to the other. St. Paul then insightfully articulates what this will mean for each, highlighting what is often our greatest weakness. He first employs the analogy that we have seen. Both men and women are to be like Christ. Men and women are made to the image of God. Period. Yet there is a further signification in our sex which we make known, visible, in creation. Men and women are natural symbols. They signify the nuptial meaning of reality and ultimately of Christ's union with his Bride, the Church. As unpopular as this may be due to abuse or misinterpretation, it is revelation and thus must carry with it only light, not darkness.

Is a woman thus to be subject to her husband in obedience? What does this mean? As a head directs, so the body moves. How can we understand this? We cannot outside the revelation of Jesus Christ. We must see it first in the ideal if we are to see it in the real. A man's movements must be like that of a dance, a *pas de deux* of a ballet, for example. Each of his movements inclines her, indicates to her, how she might move in grace and beauty, employing his strength for the purpose of her own exaltation. What woman would refuse? We are not speaking about absolute obedience but rather one that flows from his desire to elevate her.

In the garden story, Adam did not direct. He neither defended her nor intervened. He let her "spin" out of control and even consented to disobedience by his own eating of the fruit. He did not say no. His no and her acceptance of that no would have been her exaltation, not their mutual destruction. The rehabilitation in grace which takes place in marriage requires obedience because we must learn to maintain another's word. The woman must trust the man. She must, time and time again, maintain his word, call him to keep his word, inspire him to keep God's word! She must engage the sacrament which empowers her to abandon herself, to leap, as it were, into his hands, believing that they are strong and will not falter.

In turn, the price of walking hand-in-hand back to the

Father as seen in the wedding ceremony will mean sacrifice. Husbands love your wives as Christ loved the Church. Every man secretly wants to sacrifice himself for something greater. Once he wanted to be like God without God. Now God is crucified and the desire that wells up from the sacrament gives the man strength to offer his life in sacrifice.

St. Paul wittingly states that no man hates his own flesh but loves and cherishes it. He is calling him back to Adam in the beginning. "This one is flesh of my flesh!" Turn aside from the love of your own body. Your body has been sacrificed to build up woman. Your body must be sacrificed now as she builds up your children. They are your flesh which you must feed, your body which you must cherish. You are not to give yourself to yourself in some hellish caricature of your power, but rather to sacrifice yourself for them. The man kneels in the sanctuary with his bride clothed in beauty. To assist her to get home, to aid her to be "without spot or wrinkle or any such thing" will cost him his life. Nothing less is required, and anything less will be insufficient for the call of the sacrament.

Yet for this sacrament to be fruitful, the woman must in turn receive that gift as the Church receives the life of Christ. She must transform sacrifice, in the hidden recesses of her garden, into fruitfulness. Her body does this in children, but her soul must accomplish this by volition. No one can make anything live without the feminine. Sacrifice as a seed is futile without the bower of her body and soul. She is a sign of God's fecundity. He does not allow the seed that has died to remain alone, but receives it and brings forth ten, twenty, one hundred-fold.

It is only in light of the fruitfulness of the Passion, as seen in the ever-Virgin Mother herself, that this famous passage from Ephesians can be rightly understood. Christ's death was ironically the very cause of her life as the Immaculate Conception. It is he who preserved her from sin and filled her with grace. It is she who received and maintained his word, bringing forth first the fruit of his human sonship, and then at the cross the sonship of all in the order of grace. This divine and human dance of word and receptivity is far from subjection that leads to domination. It is mutual gift which leads to life and exaltation. This is the sacrament of marriage. The imperfect ways through which each couple participates in the Passion allow them to become instruments of perfecting. This transformation through the sacrament of marriage is both the grace given and the grace that is operative. Only our response limits it.

CHAPTER 6

SACRAMENT OF RESTORING DIVINE LIFE: PENANCE

VEILS AND VISIONS

If one walks into a Catholic church a couple of weeks before Easter, he or she will notice something rather strange. Near the sanctuary there appear to be shrouded sentinels. Everywhere there was a statue or crucifix there is now an eerie purple veil covering them, transforming them into faceless specters. Why does the Church do this?

Before the Second Vatican Council, it was proscribed that women wear veils in the presence of the Blessed Sacrament. Similarly, nuns along with chalices and tabernacles classically have veils. What is the purpose of all of this concealment? Is not the body something good and beautiful? Are not our images of Christ and his saints to remind us of the glory to which we strive?

St. Paul calls a woman's hair her glory (1 Cor 11:15).

There is a sense in which her glory, the beauty God has given to her, is covered when she prays. Her glory shrouded, veiled, as an image of the Bride, the Church. This glory received from God is given back to Christ in worship. But there is a further reason for which veils are connected with the Mass, particularly during that time just before Christ suffers and dies in the liturgical calendar, known as Passiontide.

Christ's glory is hidden from us in his passion. "He had no beauty or majesty to attract us to him, nothing in his appearance that we should desire him" (Is 53:2). This is symbolized in the Extraordinary Form of the Roman Rite. The paten (gold plate) and host are offered to God. The host is then laid on the linen cloth called a corporal (from the Latin for body, *corpus*). The Sacrifice of the Mass is near and the glory of God in Christ is hidden. The paten is taken away and hidden until the Passion is over. When the double consecration is finished, the sacrifice has been affected. The fruit of this sacrifice? We can now become sons and daughters of God and thus we stand and say the Our Father. His glory returns with the Resurrection, signified by the return of the golden paten. Now Christ can impart to us in the Mass his peace, as he did in the upper room after he rose. "Peace be with you." As we prepare for the glory of Easter, those signs of beauty and glory in our churches are veiled.

Once on Mt. Tabor, Christ revealed his glory to Peter, James, and John. His clothes and even his flesh became luminous, radiating a glory that the apostles had never seen. This vision has been called the cessation of a perpetual miracle. In other words, the natural effect of Christ's humanity being perfectly united to his divinity would have been the overflow of glory into the body. This flood of glory was held at bay, as it were, until this moment. Christ allows this glory to fill him, to reveal itself through him like light pouring through his very pores. He does this just before he sacrifices this flesh on the wood of the cross. These Apostles behold this glory. The image is burned into their memories and branded into their hearts as an abiding attraction to which they return when darkness falls. These same Apostles would see the transfigured face of Christ in the garden of Gethsemane when liquid glory is exchanged for the outpouring of blood.

Suffering acts like a veil. It hides the true glory of Christ, and yet that suffering ironically reveals the intensity of divine love. It was at the cross in the darkest hour that someone recognized who Christ was (Mk 15:39; Lk 23:42). No one has greater love than to lay down one's life for one's friends (Jn 15:13). Some saw this and some did not. Some see it and some do not. Christ could have manifested himself to the whole world in his transfigured beauty but chose rather the veiled glory to manifest the deepest divine love. The question is why?

"And I, when I am lifted up from the earth, will draw all men to myself" (Jn 12:32). Like iron filings to a magnet we are drawn to Christ crucified because our sins are drawn. He did not ask. Yet he assumed the sins of the world, drank them freely in the Garden, offered them in his Body on the cross, and returned what he took from us in the form of saving blood. The veil of his side was torn open and what was revealed was the Sacred Heart. Even the meanest sinner can be attracted to it. Raw glory is not ours. Beauty unalloyed is not for us. Suffering calls to us as one of our own and beckons us to its side. As we draw near to the cross, however, we will only remain if we recognize the cause. I am the cause of this.

I have drawn him down in his mad love to give what I could not, to offer what I would not. At this point, one of two things can happen: we can confess or we can run.

To receive mercy, ironically, requires an unveiling of our own. I must take off the feigned glory, the costume of comeliness. I must willfully reveal that which he sees but that which perhaps I do not. I must unveil my ugliness. I must confess. This is the nature of reconciling. *Truth must be accepted for mercy to be given.* Mercy is not the abolition of justice, but rather mercy entails that someone other than the offender pay the price of justice. The price is paid not by the offender but by the offended. We can do nothing about the offense. We cannot undo it. We can simply see it, show that we see it, unveil it, and beg forgiveness. It is up to the offended to give the gift of forgiveness.

The very words we use for forgiveness have imbedded etymologically the reality of the gift. Pardon, *perdon, perdonare, pardonner,* all speak of a gift that is given. Gifts by their nature are not required. One might say: "I did not ask God to die for me! I do not want his gift of mercy!" And you need not receive it. He offers it nonetheless. The only thing required is the unveiling of our sins and consequent sorrow. What is required is the identification with his passion, the approaching of his throne of divine love, and the opening of our heart. He veiled his glory to reveal his love; we remove our false glory to receive his mercy. Since the first sin, we have hidden from him. We must let him examine us. His searching eyes do not search out our sins for the simple purpose of shame. His purpose is not to make us run back to find fig leaves, properly chastened. On the contrary, he convicts us of sin so as to remove it and become our advocate (see Jn 16:8; 14:16). The very word *advocate* or *paraclete* means to call someone to our side, to defend us. Against whom? The accuser.

It is interesting to note how some languages deal with gifts. In English, when something is given, we say thank you, which has its roots in the verb *to think*. To think about what? To think about the gift, to see it as something worthy of gratitude. This is similar to the short hand of the romance languages which simply say "gift" or "grace" as in *gracias, grazie, gratias,* or, in the French, mercy (*merci*), or finally in the Portugese *obrigado* which comes from the Latin for being bound to someone as in obligation.

The response to this recognized gift is also interesting. Italians say prego, "I pray" (*prego* is not just a jar of sauce) which is similar to the French *je vous en prie* as a response to the *merci* just proclaimed. Latin is also quite profound. One recognizes a gift given and "recognizes" the gift by making a moral intention of its return. St. Thomas speaks of this when he discusses gratitude. We cannot often return the gift *in kind,* but we can make an internal act of gratitude that is proportionate with the gift. The response in Latin is *libenter dedi*, meaning "I gave it freely." In all of these there is nothing "taken simply for granted" but a reciprocal act by which we internally see and recognize the gift and express it in gratitude.

Forgiveness has a similar movement of recognition and donation. When I cause pain to another, my apology properly demands that I see what it was that I did. When I was a child, I recall one occasion in which my father told me to apologize to my mother. When I asked what it was that I had done, he said humorously: "It doesn't matter!" While humorous, it was not the best lesson he had ever given. Just as gratitude comes from recognition of freely given gifts, so too the request for "forgiveness" entails a capacity to know the offense. How have I hurt you? The degree to which we love another is the degree of sorrow we will have upon the vision of the crime. Only when the justifications are dried up and the pain of the other remains can we truly ask for the gift of forgiveness. The offended can have the gift prepared, but the reciprocal nature is not complete until it is seen and received.

What if you had offended someone you love in a grievous way, something malicious, something which rightly severed your relationship. Imagine further that you have no opportunity to ask or to beg for forgiveness. You are locked with a disorder. It is not just that you were wrong but that now *you* are wrong. You live in a state of debt, the payment of which you cannot make nor ask another to pay it for you in mercy. How often we forget what an incredible blessing time and space are, for they afford us the opportunity of making amends (literally to get out of fault, *ex* + *menda*). We want to be freed, loosened, untied. This our Lord has done in what is called the second plank of salvation after the shipwreck of sin. This is confession.

CHRIST'S COMMAND OF PENANCE

After his resurrection, our blessed Lord breathed on his Apostles and then proclaimed: "Receive the Holy Spirit. If you forgive the sins of any, they are forgiven; if you retain the sins of any, they are retained" (Jn 20:22–23). Like a new creation, he breathed into them divine life and with that life came a command and with that command a power. Some might ask why we should confess to a man, but we do not simply confess to a man; we confess to God. We do, however, confess *through* a man, and we do this for at least four reasons:

1. The most important reason is obedience. Christ has commanded that our sins be forgiven in this fashion. Christ's commands are most truly known when they are first obeyed.

2. Sin is veiled and hides in us and grows when its truth or reality is locked inside. Darkness cozens it. Forgetfulness absolves it from consciousness. Yet it lives a parasitic life which feeds on our interior. The truth sets us free. Light scatters darkness. When sin takes the incarnate form of articulation in confession, it is exposed to the light and seen not just by the priest but, more importantly, by ourselves.

3. Sin is not simply personal. It is communal by nature. We are not saved as individuals but as persons incorporated into a body and it is to that body which we have damaged by each sin, hidden or not, that we must reconcile.

4. As mentioned above about the reciprocal nature of forgiveness, it is not enough to confess, we must be given the gift. Our relationship with God need not be silent. We do not have to wonder whether or not he has forgiven us. He does not want us to live on such tenuous ground. Has he forgiven me for this act? This horrible crime? This wicked deed? Such is his mercy that he does not leave you in that state of not finding him, of not having space and time to plead for that gift. In other words, one of the reasons for which Christ established this as a means of imparting

his forgiveness is so that he can tell you: "I forgive you. I absolve you. I set you free. I myself pay for this debt and release you."

Sin is personal. Sin is communal. It is a person with whom we speak in confession. It is the communal life to which that person readmits us. To be sure, it is often emotionally therapeutic to speak about our sins. Yet we have all experienced the weight of our sins rushing back after the momentary relief from them has expired. We do not simply need to reveal them, we need to be rid of them, we must discharge them. This God alone can do, and he has wisely chosen to do it by this sacrament.

ELEMENTS OF THE SACRAMENT

Non-Catholics often believe that the sacrament of Penance, commonly referred to as confession, is an easy juridical exchange. Jokes abound relative to sin on Friday, confession on Saturday, communion on Sunday, repeat. But we have already noted that the sacraments are not magic. As with all of the sacraments, there are necessary elements. In this sacrament, however, the "matter" is not water, oil, bread, or wine. It is sin. Sin being brought by the sinner to the Church. The matter is man in his state matched with a man as priest. This meeting is congruent with our normal experience of reconciliation. It is personal. If a genuine reconciliation is to take place, the penitent must bring his sin, make known his sin, and not withhold purposely any grave sin. What is grave sin?

Any rudimentary catechism class will eventually make the distinction between venial and mortal sin. The word *mortal* means "death" and takes its cue from the first letter of John

5:16. Mortal sin is an offense which kills. It kills the divine life in us, aborts it, vanquishes it. We attempt to define mortal sin as something which is grave in itself, and we do it knowingly and willingly. This makes perfect sense. In any relationship, we can clearly see that some actions damage a relationship, while others sever it.

Even so, it's not always easy to see when one has sinned mortally. The effects are often slight at first as spiritual inertia keeps us moving. That motion towards divine things, the enjoyment of divine things, the internal tranquility of order, eventually loses momentum. A distaste for the spiritual life wells up inside us. Mortal sin parasitically reigns in us unchecked. These sins must be confessed in both kind and number. What did I do? How many times did I do it? God does not require a perfect memory but a contrite and humble heart. Nevertheless for the reasons enumerated above, we are charged in love to *see*. In some sense we can say that a normal physician heals only what he can see, whereas the Divine physician heals that which *we* see.

The classic scriptural text on divine forgiveness is of course the parable of the prodigal son. It is significant that the father does not follow the younger son. The son leaves with his inheritance and the father must let him go. After a time, his inertia is gone. His inheritance has run out. He is left in want. It is this recognition that moves his feet back in the direction of his father. As he rehearses what he will say, the father has already caught sight of him, as if watching for him. The father does not wait for the son to arrive. He rushes out to bridge the gap, so feverish is his love. He is more eager to bestow gifts on his son than his son is to confess. The son speaks his rehearsed lines, but the father does not even listen.

He has calves killed, clothes brought, and festivities begun. The father could not bestow these on his son until his son was able to receive them. Once he was, however, the tidal wave of his mercy crashed over him.

This movement of father and son was one to the other. They moved simultaneously. The absolution of the priest, traditionally, was said while the penitent made the act of contrition. Why? Because this is the "form" of the sacrament. In other words, just as Baptism has the sign and the corresponding determination of the words "I baptize you," so too the matter of the sacrament is sin presented with contrition (literally, "with sorrow") and the priest is saying the form "I absolve you."[18] As in the parable, the acts happen in unison.

EFFECTS OF THE SACRAMENT

These two movements, the penitent to Christ through the priest and the movement of Christ to the penitent through the priest, make up the *sacramentum* or the full sign of the sacrament which effects what it symbolizes. What does it symbolize? Yes, it symbolizes reconciliation, but the immediate effect, or the sign with its effected reality, is the movement of the heart to true contrition, what is often called interior penance. What must have happened to the son in the parable when he saw the reaction of his father? No doubt it moved his heart to even greater sorrow and purpose of amendment. "How could my father be so good? How could I have treated him so maliciously, so callously?"

It is true that we can go to confession with simple attrition

---

18   Perfect contrition, as we shall see, is not required of the penitent.

(literally, "without sorrow"). In fact, the classic "act of contrition" covers both possibilities. We can go because we do not want punishment. When I see blue lights in my rear-view mirror, I regret that I sped, but I do not have sorrow. Sorrow comes from love, and love for rational creatures is always personal. The grace of the sacrament makes it personal. It infuses divine love into us which causes the heart to have genuine sorrow.

The ultimate effect of the sacrament is the restoration of divine friendship.[19] Grace pours into the soul and the virtues are once again infused with new life. But some of the effects of our sins remain. We have created by repeated action stable dispositions toward those actions. We are sometimes shocked to find that we confess something and then return to it so quickly. Is it because we did not have a firm purpose of amendment? Possibly. More likely it is the case that we have a vice, and more is needed to curb this tendency than a confession. If I have dug a trough in my yard in which the rainwater flows, it will always flow there until I fill in the trough. I cannot simply tell the rainwater to go somewhere else when gravity takes it to the lowest point.

After our confession, the priest assigns a penance for satisfaction and healing to continue after the sacrament is finished. This penance begins the process of filling in the trough. The Lord speaks about prayer, fasting, and almsgiving as the penances that ultimately heal the soul from its communion with the world, the flesh, and the devil. The priest may assign a penance in any of these areas or other good works to be done

---

[19]   See III, q. 84, a. 1 ad 3; q. 90 a. 2; q. 85 a. 3 and 4. St Thomas states that the ultimate effect of the sacrament is *reconciliatio amicitiae*.

which begin the process of employing the grace received to root out the vice.

FRUITFULNESS OF THE SACRAMENT

To see properly, we need two things: light and love. Without proper light, we see only obscurely, confusedly. To see without love is a different kind of darkness. We don't evaluate the thing we see properly. Perhaps a better metaphor is light without heat. We need to see but we also need to be warmed. The Holy Spirit must be invoked for a fruitful confession. He, the fire of charity and the bond of love, will grant us the grace of a good confession if only we would ask him.

First, let us consider light by which to see. Who can discern his own errors? From hidden faults acquit me, O Lord (Ps 19:12). Self-knowledge is one of the most essential elements of the spiritual life. We do not see ourselves well at all. We are experts at subterfuge, even from ourselves. Silence, recollection, examination, and an uncompromising fidelity to the truth about ourselves is required for true self-knowledge. Yet we are not alone in the examination. We have our advocate. When a painting is in a darkened room, it may appear flawless. So too does the soul whose conscience is darkened by sin. St. Thomas says that the darkness of the intellect is one of the worst effects of sin because the spiritually blind are bound to fail.

The approach of the Holy Spirit is a flood of light. Imperfections are quickly seen like a painting brought into full sun. Rabbit holes of twisted volition are explored. Locked rooms of the heart are thrown open. The past is dredged and sins which do not get forgiven by time float to the surface of consciousness. To the extent that we yield, to the extent that we pray, we are slowly brought into all truth. When we stand before his throne, we do not want surprises. It is better we should see all things now as they truly stand. To wait until death is to make yourself mute and paralyzed to repent.

But this light not only shines on us. It shines on him. The Spirit's love for him enlightens us as to his appearance, his indescribable goodness, and his crushing love. The light of self-knowledge can be a cause of despair if it were not matched by the attractive heat of his love. He draws us. These two movements in us are the cause of true purification. Come to me, says the Lord, "Though your sins are like scarlet, / they shall be as white as snow; / though they are red like crimson, / they shall become like wool" (Is 1:18). The process of turning crimson sins into incandescent love is ironically done by the blood of the Lamb. The application of his blood not on doorposts or on goats but on souls is the work of the sacraments. Baptism is the first washing, confession the rewashing. St. Ambrose stated that there are two waters, the waters of Baptism and the tears of repentance.[20] This second bath, the waters of repentance, require first sight of sin and then sight of him. This process by which we see and are crushed, see him and are impelled by love, is purgatorial.

In John Henry Cardinal Newman's poem *The Dream of Gerontius*, a man who has died is "carried" by his guardian angel to the judgment seat. After some time has "passed" in the interval of his death and their current passage, he asks why he has not yet arrived at the throne of God. He thought the Church taught that the particular judgment was immediate. After explaining the alteration of time on that side of the

---

[20]   *Catechsim of the Catholic Church,* no. 1429.

veil, the angel cautions him as to his wish. In this he explains (through the words of the angel) perfectly the dual nature of light and heat, truth and love, that is given to us in proper preparation for confession by the Holy Spirit:

> When then—if such thy lot—thou seest thy Judge,
> The sight of Him will kindle in thy heart
> All tender, gracious, reverential thoughts.
> Thou wilt be sick with love, and yearn for Him,
> And feel as though thou couldst but pity Him,
> That one so sweet should e'er have placed Himself
> At disadvantage such, as to be used
> So vilely by a being so vile as thee.
> There is a pleading in His pensive eyes
> Will pierce thee to the quick, and trouble thee.
> And thou wilt hate and loathe thyself; for, though
> Now sinless, thou wilt feel that thou hast sinn'd, {360}
> As never thou didst feel; and wilt desire
> To slink away, and hide thee from His sight:
> And yet wilt have a longing aye to dwell
> Within the beauty of His countenance.
> And these two pains, so counter and so keen,—
> The longing for Him, when thou seest Him not;
> The shame of self at thought of seeing Him,—
> Will be thy veriest, sharpest purgatory. (#360)

When the soul catches sight of him, it flies out of the grasp of the angel, propelled by love alone. Yet these two pains, the longing for him and the shame at seeing him, burn him in his flight. Again, from the angel:

> Praise to His Name!
> The eager spirit has darted from my hold,
> And, with the intemperate energy of love,

Flies to the dear feet of Emmanuel;
But, ere it reach them, the keen sanctity,
Which with its effluence, like a glory, clothes
And circles round the Crucified, has seized,
And scorch'd, and shrivell'd it; and now it lies
Passive and still before the awful Throne.
O happy, suffering soul! for it is safe,
Consumed, yet quicken'd, by the glance of God. (#366)

The book of Revelation states that nothing impure can live in the presence of God. Praise to his name indeed that he has given us this sacrament of his divine fire of love to purify us and restore us to his love. Frequent confession, when aided by the grace of the Holy Spirit, will not breed guilt and shame, but rather true self-knowledge, a desire for conversion, and an increase in strength against temptation. What wondrous love is this? We speak and he speaks. Our words meet his like the son on the road and the father rushing down it. What a mingling! Incarnate words of sin confessing and Incarnate crucified love professing that you are once again his.

CHAPTER 7

SACRAMENT OF DIVINE LIFE HEALED: ANOINTING OF THE SICK

LIVING ON THE BORDER

It has been noted that 40 percent of the Gospels are concerned with one thing: Christ's passion, death, and resurrection. Why so much concentration on one week of his life? Perhaps because it is for this purpose, he says, that he has come. To be "baptized" by his self-offering.

Christ's death is that which gives us the possibility of eternal life. Yet a cursory glance at the rest of the Gospel passages will also reveal that Christ is frequently engaged in healing. The two things are inextricably linked. Ageing, sickness, and suffering are but the harbingers of death. The power of Christ over sickness and death is attested to on many occasions. He not only heals but also raises the dead. It is no more difficult for him to raise someone from the dead than it is for us to wake one from sleep. He simply commands, *talitha koum*, "get up little girl," or to his friend, "Lazarus come forth" (Mk 5:41; Jn 11:43). What is not so easy, however, is for Christ to raise us from eternal death; to forgive our sins and bring us to life cost him his life.

In the fifth chapter of Luke, we read:

> On one of those days, as he was teaching, there were Pharisees and teachers of the law sitting by, who had come from every village of Galilee and Judea and from Jerusalem; and the power of the Lord was with him to heal. And behold, men were bringing on a bed a man who was paralyzed, and they sought to bring him in and lay him before Jesus; but finding no way to bring him in, because of the crowd, they went up on the roof and let him down with his bed through the tiles into the midst before Jesus. And when he saw their faith he said, "Man, your sins are forgiven you." And the scribes and the Pharisees began to question, saying, "Who is this that speaks blasphemies? Who can forgive sins but God only?" When Jesus perceived their questionings, he answered them, "Why do you question in your hearts? Which is easier, to say, 'Your sins are forgiven you,' or to say, 'Rise and walk'? But that you may know that the Son of man has authority on earth to forgive sins"—he said to the man who was paralyzed—"I say to you, rise, take up your bed and go home." And immediately he rose before them, and took up that on which he lay, and went home, glorifying God. And amazement seized them all, and they glorified God and were filled with awe, saying, "We have seen strange things today." (Lk 5:17–26)

A paralyzed man is lowered through a roof. A man's sins are forgiven which God alone can do. A man is healed and walks away. Strange things indeed!

Yet we should break this scene down. Were the friends of the paralyzed man seeking to have his sins forgiven or looking for healing? I do not think the friends were attempting to send him to confession. They wanted physical healing. They wanted him to walk. Similarly, we do not often want to be saved from sin. We usually seek to be saved from suffering. In this scene, Christ does not seem to even notice the physical suffering. His eye focuses immediately on the sin since sin is his main concern and the purpose for which he came. St. John the Baptist knew this: "Behold, the Lamb of God, who takes away the sin of the world" (Jn 1:29). Bodily suffering is not the central problem. Physical death is not even the essential problem. The malady that Christ sees and comes to heal is the decaying spiritual life. A gangrenous soul is what he sees, touches, and heals. He looks at the paralytic and says: "Your sins are forgiven."

Christ's accusers call his actions blasphemous. He, in turn, asks them a question which is the strangest of all: "Which is easier to say?" In fact, it is *easier* to say your sins are forgiven. But how can one tell? The effect of sin in the soul is not something one can sense. It is true we *do* feel the effects of sin as we *do* feel the effects of forgiveness. Yet who can *see* this? In truth, it is much more difficult to say "get up and walk" because that is an object of our senses. If the man were not to get up, Christ would be exposed as a charlatan. Yet the man does, in fact, rise and walk.

The irony that makes this passage intriguing is that while it is easier for *us* to say "your sins are forgiven" since it has no external verifiable sign, it is actually harder for Christ to say your sins are forgiven. To make the man's body rise requires a simple command of divine power. To make the soul rise to new life is to forgive sins. Forgiving sins is effected by Christ's death. To forgive one sin as man is to ignite his passion and death. To heal a soul is to embrace the cross.

Why didn't Christ heal everyone? Why didn't he cause all to rise? Because suffering and death would be employed by Christ, not vanquished. The wage of sin, St. Paul asserts, is death (Rom 6:23). It is this "wage" that Christ received. It is this wage that we will all receive. Yet suffering and death have now been transformed by the One who went before us. It is not annihilation. In Christ it is the moment of victory.

The French author George Bernanos once stated that it was not his life that he should strive to make happy and beautiful, but rather his death. Death is the point of convergence and consummation of a life. If that is not done well, nothing else really matters. To this end, one must see himself die. The ancient practice of the *memento mori* (which literally means "remember to die") was the habit of watching oneself die so as to positively affect the time of living. The *ars moriendi,* or the "art of dying," is not "morbid" in the sense that it refers strictly to things diseased. The art of dying is rationally looking with clear honesty at ourselves who carry the disease. What *is* morbid is me. I am diseased and I need healing. To diagnose the disease is necessary for its eradication. Decomposition is the result of distraction and delusion, not of inspection. While a doctor can heal only that which he sees, Christ the physician heals only that which you have come to see.

I must live conscious of the border on which I live. I am a liminal creature. I live on the threshold of eternity every second. *Memento mori.* Euphemisms will do us no good. One does not "pass away." One does not "look good" in the coffin. One does not get placed into a "memorial park" but a cemetery.

The word *cemetery*, however, might help us understand something deeper, since it comes from the Greek for lying down to sleep. It was employed by the Christians to distinguish their death from the pagan understanding. We can be "woken" by Christ just as Lazarus was. Christ even said, "I go to wake him." He wakes us not to a continuation of our earthly life but unto a new heavens and a new earth. In that sense, each sleep is a dress rehearsal. We lie down each night in the hope of waking in the morning just as we die in the hope of waking to eternal life. All suffering and even death can now be united to his passion and thus become for me, and you, a remedy. As sleep is a yielding of the body to weakness, so too we yield to suffering and death, we endure it as the very means which attacks our pride, our self-reliance, our egoism. This, and only this, turns suffering from meaninglessness to glorified dignity. In Christ, death no longer has power over life. There is only One who has come back from the dead. Only One who has conquered it. What hope is ours in Christ when we die before we die! What hope of making death a true *ars*, a true art, by delivering ourselves not into the hands of annihilation but into his hands. To live on the border and to gaze into the "undiscovered country" with one's foot in forward motion is, for the Christian, the way to walk into everlasting life.

The wages of suffering and death will be received by each of us. While the Christian finds in them both meaning and ultimate healing of soul, it is nevertheless true that Christ did heal the body. Healing, too, was a means to an end, namely, drawing out the faith of the recipient as well as those who witnessed it. Similarly, Christ entrusted this healing activity to his Apostles. They were allowed to heal with oil before they were empowered to heal the soul with absolution (see Mk 6:13). In some sense, they were practicing the art. Healing was a charismatic gift given to them to do the works that Christ himself did. The charismatic gift of healing was crystallized into a sacrament by Christ's injunction to his Apostles to "heal the sick." We call it the sacrament of the Anointing of the Sick. The way in which Christ healed, however, is the way he heals now. He heals the spiritual and in his inscrutable will for our good, sometimes the body is healed. The latter, however, is always at the service of the former.

ELEMENTS OF THE SACRAMENT

As the sacrament of Anointing is tied to the forgiveness of sins, so is it tied to the priesthood as the servant of Christ's passion. In the letter of St. James we read: "Is any among you sick? Let him call for the elders of the Church, and let them pray over him, anointing him with oil in the name of the Lord; and the prayer of faith will save the sick man, and the Lord will raise him up; and if he has committed sins, he will be forgiven" (Jas 5:14–15).

This very text makes its way into the actual rite of the sacrament. It is the office of the priest to offer. In St. Matthew's Gospel, the very specific word for a Temple offering is employed when the sick are brought to Jesus. Those sicknesses are "offerings" which he alone can accept and transform into something pleasing to God. Therefore the priest, who acts in the Person of Christ, is sent to that very moment of con-summation in the individual's life, to consecrate the sufferings and give them to Christ so that he might unite them to his sacrifice.

What gesture is employed for this offering of sacrifice to Christ? Once again, we see the laying on of hands. This priestly gesture marks out the body for sacrifice in its extrem-ity. The *ars moriendi* is reaching its final stroke when the fresco of the Passion is painted in the suffering supple flesh of the Christian. Oil is the matter employed as a sign of healing. It receives the further signature of designation by the words: "Through this holy anointing, may the Lord in his love and mercy help you with the grace of the Holy Spirit." While say-ing this, the priest traces a cross with the oil on the forehead. He continues by saying: "May the Lord who frees you from sin, save you and raise you up." These words are accompanied by similar crosses drawn with oil on the palms of the hands.

The rite as it was celebrated prior to the Second Vatican Council was more visceral in its wording and gestures:

> In the name of the Father, + and of the Son, + and of the Holy + Spirit; may any power the devil has over you be destroyed by the laying-on of our hands and by calling on the glorious and blessed Virgin Mary, Mother of God, her illustrious spouse, St. Joseph, and all holy angels, archangels, patriarchs, prophets, apos-tles, martyrs, confessors, virgins, and all the saints.

The priest then proceeded to anoint all of the senses with the cross, asking for forgiveness for the ways each of the senses had been the occasion of sin. For example:

By this holy anointing + and by His most tender mercy may the Lord forgive you all the evil you have done through the power of sight.

Each of the senses receives the same request. The senses are like highways of material traffic becoming five different avenues from our interior to the exterior and return. As such, they are each in need of healing.

EFFECTS OF THE SACRAMENT

What can be seen from the signs? They both accomplish the same end but with a slightly different emphasis. The latter form highlights the body's preparation as an offering, not for destruction, but for glorification. What the new rite seems to highlight more is the cleansing of the mind symbolized by the forehead and the cleansing of one's deeds symbolized by the hands. The intellect and the will are cleansed not only of actual sin but what is called temporal punishment due to sin. Sin has effects. It leaves its fingerprints, so to speak, onto matter. Volition (the act of willing) is a spiritual reality. It moves us toward an end that we see. This movement is acted out in matter.

Consider, for example, difficult domestic life. None of us are yet saints and thus our children must grow in an environment that is not perfect. The extent to which this imperfection is sinful is to some degree the extent that the child suffers tendencies toward evil. The volition of parents is "kneaded" into the characters of their children. In some ways, we spend the rest of our lives attempting to act instead of react to that which is simply *in us* by family of origin. While sin can be forgiven, the effects of it remain. For that, we need to make *amends*. Penance is that act of justice by which we volitionally make a conscience decision to attempt to work with grace. The metal of nature must be fired and hammered to its proper beauty and form. Whether that distortion was created by another's acts of volition or our own sinful choices, the way back is the same. When, however, we can no longer move and no longer act, when we are in true danger of death, that is when Christ comes to heal us through his Church.

Anointing is like the final purgatorial scenes in Dante's *Divine Comedy*. In the final chapter of the *Purgatorio,* Dante has purged his sins by ascending to the heights of the mountain. Nevertheless, he still is made to pass through two rivers after the remnants of sin have all been reordered by the forge of penance. As a molten blade that must be cooled and tempered after the heat of the forge, so does his intensely purged soul find refreshment and completion here. This process tempers him and prepares him for heaven. The first river is "Lethe" (Greek for "forgetfulness") which washes his memory of his mortal sins. The second river is named "Eunoe," meaning "good mind." Dante must drink this water to wash his mind and refresh it, as that mind is soon to be filled with the light of heaven. He is being prepared for the vision of God. The *Purgatory* ends with these words: *puro e disposto a salire a le stelle,* "pure and prepared to climb to the stars."

FRUITFULNESS OF THE SACRAMENT

In some sense, one does not "live" this sacrament on this side of the veil. It is administered when one is in danger of death. The first effect is to consecrate those sufferings so as to be meritorious for the one suffering and those he or she loves.

It incorporates suffering into the Mystical Body through that one who now offers it in readiness. Thus, fortitude, patience, and humility are animated by the sacrament. While the priest is the one who administers the sacrament, the suffering soul is the one who offers the sacrifice. This means that the fruitfulness is found principally in acceptance. We do not simply resign ourselves but rather we offer ourselves. It is not simply passive but active. Sometimes bodily health is restored. More often one shoulders the cross with the nobility of a Christian.

The ultimate effect, like that just described in Dante's *Divine Comedy*, is not lived in this life but is transitional for the life to come. One of the great blessings offered at the end of the sacrament is what is commonly called *Holy Viatium*. This simple Latin word means "to go with you." What do you take on this journey? No walking staff, no money belt, no sandals. One thing alone are we allowed at that liminal moment. Him. We take him. Viaticum is our final Holy Communion. He who alone has conquered death is placed on our tongue, descends to our souls, and abides with us as we cross the border.

CHAPTER 8

SACRAMENT OF IMPARTING DIVINE LIFE: HOLY ORDERS

ELECTION

If we look objectively at the life of our Blessed Lord, we see a certain selectivity that is the prerogative of all love. When speaking about human love, St. Thomas notes that the word *dilectio* (one of the words for love in Latin) has imbedded in it the notion of election. Love is not for mankind but for this man and this woman. Human love requires a choice. One can be moved by the goodness he or she sees in another, whether physical or spiritual. Nevertheless, to love another is to *will* good to the other; to want the other to exist and to live; to want the other to thrive.

To the extent that we love others, we are willing to labor for their good, even to suffer in proportion to our love for them. Yet one does not will good as a distant admirer. We want to participate in the life of the other, to hold a common life.

Love is not "disinterested." Love wants to rejoice in the company of the other, to delight in the concordance of wills. The elixir of love shared is the eradication of enclosed solitude when one can say to another, "You too?" A friend classically defined is another self. One is not absorbed into the other. Each must remain "other" and yet be united as "another." Genuine friendship with many is not possible for reasons of space, time, and temperament. As the Scriptures state, when one finds a friend, he finds a treasure (see Sir 6:14).

Our Blessed Lord was exceptionally selective with his friendships. We know little to nothing about his thirty years of hidden life, except that he spent it with those chosen, namely, the Blessed Mother and St. Joseph. We have not been granted access to their interior domestic life. Neither Christ in his revelation nor Our Lady in her recounting opened the window onto their intimate life. Those stones of Loreto might whisper but they do not speak. What we have been granted, however, is a glimpse into the nature of our Lord's life for three years.

What do we see? From the beginning, he chose his companions carefully. Many went out to him, but not all remained with him. We know he loved Lazarus, Martha, and Mary particularly. We know he chose twelve. They would be his and he would speak of them with tenderness the night before he died when praying to his Father.

None of this means Christ does not have an infinite and specific love for all the souls for whom he died. Quite the contrary. Nevertheless, Christ as man chose only twelve men. He invited them into human bonds of fellowship that lead ultimately to Divine friendship. To twelve alone did he entrust the mysteries of his kingdom. Twelve alone did he invest with

Divine power. Twelve alone did he invite to share the daily existence of his journey. They slept on the same ground, ate the same food, and spoke privately with him once the crowds had departed. They were witnesses, not to one miracle, but to them all. To the twelve, he revealed his secrets. This is proper to friendship since friends are joined by a union of affection such that two hearts seem to be as one. Thus, one does not seem to have dismissed from his own heart that which he has placed in the heart of his friend. Christ is the door of divinity who conducts us into inner rooms; that is to say, the deep secrets of God.

Normal friendship is founded upon a certain similitude. When persons reveal themselves, one to another, a likeness is discovered and friendship can ensue. In this case, Christ did not need to discover what was in the heart of his friends. He read them. Ironically, Christ would read "out loud," articulating to each what was in his own heart. This is a characteristic of God alone. As seen in the passage of the woman at the well, she recognizes this man as the Christ because "he told me everything I have ever done" (Jn 4:29). It is both the office and the sign of divinity to manifest the secrets of another's heart. Man sees the appearance, but the Lord looks into the heart.

It is, therefore, not casually but perilously that one approaches this "friend." He *knows* you. There is no hiding. Sin can have no part with him. He sees it and because of love wants to eradicate it. As much as the Apostles might have wanted to turn back, they were irresistibly drawn to him. St. Peter can say both "Depart from me O Lord for I am a sinful man" as well as "Where should we go? You alone have the words of eternal life."

For these first friends who were chosen and who in turn chose to participate in this light, Christ's human companionship was a source of great consolation. With such few words, Christ drew these men to himself. Those who would stand by him in his time of trial were deeply attached to him, professing their capacity to die with him. While they were growing in their knowledge of him through his revelation, it is nevertheless true that their friendship with him, while noble, was naturally dependent upon Christ's human presence. Our Lord will test them with periodic absences to prepare them for a different kind of presence that will not be dependent upon mere physical proximity or human affection but on the complete identification of his Person with them as priests.

One such occasion is found in chapter six of John's Gospel. It was the first time that our Lord went up onto the mountain alone without informing the disciples of where he was. He had left them. They waited until evening, but so great was their love, says St. Thomas, that they could wait no longer and went in search of him. As long as the disciples enjoyed Christ's physical presence, no troubles disturbed them, nor bitterness vexed them. When they were in his company, they could cry out with the psalmist: "I said in my prosperity: / 'I shall never be moved.' / By your favor, O Lord, / you had established me as a strong mountain" (Ps 30:6–7). Such was their confidence in his presence. But when he left them, the Psalm line continued: "You hid your face, / I was dismayed" (v. 7). When he was away, be it that night or during the greater night of the Passion, the Apostles were plunged into a sea of sorrow. He had come to be their life. If he were not, they were not.

The Master offers his disciples this test preparing them for a time in which they would have him in the flesh no longer. Christ was the world around which they revolved. His absence bred inactivity and anxiety, diffusing itself in a rousing search. This love, while great, was not yet perfect, which will be made manifest during Christ's passion. When his physical presence was taken from them, it was like the removal of the sun, as all was shrouded in darkness. The hour of the Passion had come. It was no longer a time for speaking. It was a time for suffering. Before they would encounter such suffering, however, he would fortify them with the gift of himself, conforming them to himself beyond all bonds of friendship. If a friend is another self, this Friend makes them like unto himself; that is, a living sacrifice.

On the night before he died, before he gives himself to them at the Last Supper under the appearances of bread and wine, Christ does something sacramental. He uses a sign to manifest to them that which he is imparting to them. He washes their feet. Did he go through this ritual for the purpose of manifesting the simple humble service we should give one to another? On the contrary, if that were so, there would have been no need to ask the question: "Do you know what I have done for you?" What he has done in symbol was what he had done in the Incarnation and what he would do again in the Passion. Christ laid aside his robes, girded himself with a towel, bent down, and washed their feet. Finally, he resumed his garments and sat down. In the Incarnation, Christ stripped himself of glory, assumed our humanity, and wrapped himself in the mortality of the tomb. The pouring of water in the basin is symbolic of his blood by which he washes away our sins (Rv 1:5). He would rise from such labor, thus taking up again his vestment of glory and finally ascend to sit at the right hand of the Father.

In the midst of this action, however, there is the response of Peter, who, knowing himself to be a "sinful man" (Lk 5:8), refuses to be washed by Christ. Peter's intense love for Christ prompts him to make this refusal. He pays no attention to the words of the Lord, that what he is doing they will not understand now (Jn13:7). Yet Christ responds by stating that if Peter does not allow this washing, he cannot participate in Christ's life. He can have no "part with him." He cannot be his priest, his mediator. The Apostles must be conformed to Christ's passion and become the mediators of that laver of salvation. Peter's humility is turned into ardent desire, wanting to participate completely in Christ, which prompts him to beg for full immersion into the passion of the Lord. He did not know any more than James and John to what he was really requesting.

The priest is a friend of Christ's. All love is a kind of friendship. This particular kind of friendship, however, is to be like Christ in conformity to his passion. It was seen in the Anointing of the Sick that Christ's actions of healing were continued by him instrumentally in this sacrament. So too elected friendship with Christ continued as a sacrament. On the night before he died, Christ told his friends: "Greater love has no man than this, that a man lay down his life for his friends" (Jn 15:13). This he did. This they would do as well. This is the sacrament of Holy Orders.

MADE FOR THE MASS

The entire sacrament is ordered toward the Eucharist and prepares the faithful to participate in the sacrifice. "This is my body which will be given up for you." This he says of his body. This the priest repeats. For a priest to act in the person of Christ (*in persona Christi*), it must be true. He is conformed to Christ with an indelible character to make it so. The priest is a friend sacramentally and objectively. He must also be one subjectively. In other words, if he is conformed to Christ ontologically, yet not friend also by love, he becomes a living and monstrous contradiction. This is the reality. Infinite goodness united to finite weakness and, at times, wickedness. The latter is seen in the character of Judas. When Christ gives his Apostles power, it is a power they can also wield against him if they so choose.

In the sixth chapter of St. John's Gospel, when the crowds all leave Christ because of his teaching on the Holy Eucharist, a deeper betrayal is taking place. Christ himself alludes to it: "Did I not choose you, the Twelve, and one of you is a devil?" John comments on this, stating, "He spoke of Judas the son of Simon Iscariot, for he, one of the Twelve, was to betray him" (Jn 6:70–71).

The most intimate gift of himself was rejected. Judas would not keep this word. From that moment on, he stepped out of friendship with Christ. On the night of the last supper, when Christ tells them that one of them is about to betray him, he signals this betrayal by handing Judas a morsel; bread dripping with wine, given to the mouth of Judas as a kind of ceremonial communion, was the sign indicating the betrayer. He would eat bread and drink wine from the hand of Christ, but he would not accept the body and blood. He would refuse to be like Christ in the sacrifice of the cross. He would refuse his friendship. When he had taken the morsel, the text says that Satan entered into him, and it was night.

Christ's gesture of friendship was not feigned. To the last, he did not withdraw his election. "Did I not choose you?" In the garden, Judas would approach Christ. It was their final encounter. Christ began the encounter with the word *friend*. "Oh friend why are you here?" Why do you come to betray me? Why with torch and sword against the One who chose you? The kiss of Judas was no doubt a sign for others that could be recognized in the half-light of torch fire. It was a dark deed done for wicked eyes. Christ allows himself to be treated this way, yet marvels himself at the deed: "You would betray me with a kiss?" (Lk 22:48).

St. John the Baptist is a contrast to the character of Judas. John is called both friend and groomsman. This is an apt image of the priest. What is accomplished by the true spouse is first initiated by the groomsman. John prepares the bride out of love for his friend. While John possesses the humility requisite for this friendship, not considering himself worthy to unstrap the Lord's sandals, he nevertheless considers himself a true friend.

What makes this example interesting is that the Scriptures do not mention any human contact between John and our Lord (aside from the Visitation when they are both shrouded in the wombs of their mothers) upon which friendship would have been established. Mystically, John heard the approach of the Word hearing Mary's word to Elizabeth. He receives the coming of the Word with joy and exults in the womb. From that moment forward, John would keep Christ's word. He would prepare the way for him and prepare the bride for him by the preaching of the word. John rejoiced in the good of the Lord, not attempting to take the bride for himself but rather preparing her for his friend and finding in that his own joy. His perfect obedience forges in him a concordance with

Christ. He longs to hear his voice approaching. Upon hearing that union of wills, he erupts in joy (see Jn 3:29–30).

As a friend of the truth who is Christ, John bore testimony. His testimony was a light shining in the darkness. He himself was not the light but participated in the true light. So powerful was John's participation that some had put their end in John, confusing him for the true light. He had to protest that he was not the light. Just as the morning star goes before the sun to prepare its way, only to be rendered invisible by the rising of the sun, so too John, whose light was partial precisely as participated, would not be seen when the fullness of light shone. His *decrease* upon Christ's *increase* was consummated in the perfection of charity when, ironically, he offered his life in testimony to lawful marriage. What might have seemed an insignificant rubric was, for this beloved groomsman, worth the shedding of his blood.

Finally, we see this pattern fulfilled in the life of St. Peter. Love is perfect when one exposes himself to death for a friend. Peter boldly vows to lay down his life for his friend (Jn 13:37). Peter did not lie. He simply could not see that he was incapable as of yet. Man, Aquinas states, does not know the strength of his own love until met with imminent danger. The measure of love is proportionate to the suffering we are willing to endure for the beloved. Peter's love was great, but it was checked at the door of death. The border of self-sacrifice was patrolled by fear and the instinct of self-preservation. He did not want his blessed friend and master to die, nor did he desire to die himself. A friend desires the presence of the other, of shared life. Nothing is so becoming of friendship than friends living together. Nothing so obviously destroys human friendship as dying. Friendship naturally wants the other to be, to exist, to live. One fights ferociously against the death of the friend just as one would rebel against his own.

Yet Christ spoke of his death as a death for the sake of his Apostles. This incongruity only makes sense in the light of the Resurrection, which they did not yet understand. Left with no choice but to enjoy Christ's presence even unto death, Peter boasts of a love beyond his capacity. "You would give your life for me?" Christ asks. Christ knows what is in Peter, and the perfection of love is not to be found there . . . but it will be.

Peter will deny Christ with a vehemence equal to his prior profession. He cowers at the questions of those who would identify him with Christ, the very thing he was conformed to do. As Peter's love grew cold by a gripping fear, he warmed himself by a charcoal fire. Each interrogation only intensified his denials. The cock crowed, Jesus looked at him, and neither opened their mouths. Peter wept.

Perfect love casts out fear (1 Jn 4:18). After the Resurrection and the appearance in the upper room, Peter returned to the beginning. It was while fishing that Peter first encountered the Lord, and it was to that place he would return. Could there have been for Peter a memory more potent? The smell of the sea, the listing of the boat, the wet nets coursing through his hands, all these were braided memories of that first encounter. He no longer feared. The Lord had risen, and thus there was no more need of fear. But Peter had yet to be forgiven. The beloved disciple recognized the Lord on the shore, and this confirmed for Peter what he must have already known but dared to believe. At that moment, Peter's passionate devotion for Christ propelled him to spring into the water, the boat being so much slower than his desire.

Yet he is brought up short on the shore, seeing the charcoal fire, signifying the burning charity of Christ who immolated himself rather than the fire at which Peter had warmed himself. Having fed and refreshed his disciples, the Lord turns to Peter. St. Thomas views this scene as an examination of a prelate or priest before he assumes his office. The questions of the examination, Thomas notes, are simply about love. These questions are appropriate for the office Peter will assume since many who assume the pastoral office use it for their own ends. Forgiveness is wrought by charity but demands the knowledge and contrition for it to be received. Peter thus retracts his denials, one by one, with professions of love. Thomas quotes Augustine, stating that a threefold profession was required so that Peter's tongue might show as much love as it had shown of fear, and that life present before him in the beloved Christ would elicit more words than the threat of death.

Finally, the humbled Peter is afraid to boast, as he once did in the upper room. He is fearful that the Lord knows he will deny him again. In his sadness, Peter confesses that the Lord knows everything and knows what it means when he professes his love. They both know. He loves Christ indeed, and yet, would that love falter again in the face of death? Peter is no longer so confident. Peter no longer interprets the power of his love but allows the words "I love you" to be interpreted by the one whose friend he is, the one who knows the heart of Peter better than Peter himself.

Having rehabilitated Peter with these questions, the Lord prophesies about Peter's future. This time, however, the prophecy does not contain a prediction of his denials but a prediction of the form Peter's love would take. In a role reversal, it is Christ who now confesses that Peter will give his life for him. Charity will reach the zenith of perfection in Peter, the apotheosis of friendship, in giving his life for his Divine friend. Peter lived in his youth by the dictates of his own desire, clothing himself and walking where he would. But the clothing of charity will lead Peter to where he does not wish (prior to perfect charity) to go. His self-will shall conform itself to the will of Christ.

After the model of Christ, Peter will stretch out his hands in crucifixion, testifying to his friend with the power of charity, elevating and perfecting his love that previously was too feeble. Thus did Peter glorify God, and thus is he truly considered a friend of Christ. His feet were cleansed of disordered passions, of disordered self-love, and of attachment to his earthly life. His love was stronger than death, and indeed, on the other side of death. Peter, with love girded and steps directed, would walk freely as a friend where he had previously not wanted to go. The love of Christ compelled him, and he walked to his eternal home rejoicing, with his feet, ironically, in the air (according to tradition, Peter was crucified upside down).

ELEMENTS OF THE SACRAMENT

The sign of the sacrament, much like marriage, is a person. A man is chosen by Christ, and as a man, he is to act in the person of Christ. During the ordination rite, the man throws himself onto the ground while the Church prays and beseeches the saints to intercede. This plaintive cry is prompted by what we have already seen. No man, as Hebrews states, takes this on himself but only as chosen (Heb 5:4). Even as chosen will he fail? Indubitably. What he is approaching will always be both united to him and infinitely more than him. It is thus that he prostrates, offering his life in exchange for Christ's life. He prostrates as a sign that he, with the grace of God, will have the capacity of Peter to witness to Christ. He prays that he would not become a grotesque caricature but mediate the sacrifice of Christ as one who sacrifices his own life for Christ in exchange. The priest authentically states, "This is my body," referring to Christ's body. Christ can, in turn, state, "This is my body," referring to the man who is the instrument he employs. In other words, the man belongs to Christ. He is consecrated to him and no one can snatch him out of Christ's hand.

The man rises and the sacrament begins with the silent laying on of hands by the bishop. As seen before, laying on of hands marks something out for sacrifice. This is essential to the sacrament. The consecratory prayer or form gives this sign a further designation. After recounting the types of the priesthood in the history of salvation, the bishop begs God to give this man "the dignity of the priesthood."

The man is a priest. He has the character indelible for all eternity. He is a priest forever in the line of Melchizedek. He is clothed with the priestly garments, each having its own significance: the amice for the helmet of salvation, alb for the sign of baptism washed in the blood of the Lamb, cincture for the girding of our passions in service of the Lord, stole as a sign of Christ's authority, chasuble as a sign of being covered in Christ's charity; that is, his friendship. Finally, the priest's hands are anointed with chrism. His hands are then wrapped in a cloth as if they had been seared and are awaiting healing. The hands are the hands of priests, Christ's hands now by which he sanctifies his people with his blessings. They now mark out for sacrifice that which is to be offered unto the High Priest.

EFFECTS OF THE SACRAMENT

Baptism and Confirmation both confer on the recipient a character. Character ordains one to divine worship, enabling one to receive gifts and to participate in those gifts. The priesthood is specifically for the purpose of administering these crucial gifts. The very name priest in Latin means a giver of holy things. He is conformed to Christ in such a way that mediates as a friend of the Bridegroom who prepares the Bride. He prepares the Church to participate in the passion of the Lord.

This character makes of him a living instrument. The flowing power does not simply come through him when administering the sacraments but rather remains in him always. Recall that Christ's humanity was a conjoined instrument. It is substantially united to his Person as the Son of God. This is a bit like the way in which my hand is at once me and also something I use, for example, to write. It is the instrument or organ with which I write. That *through* which I write is like the pen. This is similar with the priesthood. Yet in this case, to employ the analogy, *Christ picks up a man and never lets him go.* His promise is eternal. Once raised, the man is a priest forever. To receive a power to that which is beyond your nature as a man is not, in the words of C. S. Lewis, like teaching a horse to run faster. It is like teaching a horse to fly.

The power or *vis* that the priest has is specifically the power to sanctify. He teaches and governs as that which flows from his position relative to divine worship. He does not govern in *all* things, but in those which care for the Bride, the Church. He governs her preparation for an encounter with Christ the Bridegroom. He does not teach all things but specifically those prophetic things Christ has revealed, speaking to the others what he himself has received. The priest is by nature traditional, for he does not give his own word but hands on (*tradere*) the Word Himself. Teaching and governing are for the purpose of the sanctifying office. It is here that the priest is "father" *par excellence*. He is the instrument for generating divine life, strengthening and nourishing it, restoring it and healing it. He acts as "another Christ" which is why friendship with Christ is necessary for his own sanctification. When he administers the sacraments, they are effected despite his state of unworthiness. Nevertheless, the sacraments call for worthiness, they call for love, they demand friendship for the full flourishing of his priesthood.

FRUITFULNESS OF THE SACRAMENT

The priest's autonomy has been handed over in the laying down of his life. He is a conduit of divine life, not of his own life. He does not give himself to the people (signified by his chastity) but gives himself to the service of Christ. It is love for Christ that compels him. The faithful will not grow with the nourishment of his life but that of Christ's through him. The priest must decrease while our Lord increases. The moon is but a sign of the sun's presence, but it is the sun that is the source of light. The priest must rejoice in the approach of the Bridegroom to the souls of those to whom he ministers. He does not look into them to see his own image but that of the

Bridegroom. This does not mean that he does not love them. As a mediator, he holds the Bride's hand, leading her to the Bridegroom with his eyes always looking for his approach. Why this mediation?

Men do not communicate spiritually. Our greatest concepts and our deepest longings are all communicated though matter, through gesture, through sign. Christ acts still through his humanity and through a man, sinful as he may be. Faith in the priesthood despite the failures of men is rather astounding. As one who belongs to the sacerdotal brotherhood, I can admit that as a family we are not always so inspiring. I am at least certain that I am not always inspiring. Yet weakness is also employed by Christ. He acts through the priest far beyond the man's capacities. He says things a man could not say, and does things a man could not do. The man himself is aware of this transaction going on in him and it is a deep cause of wonder.

For example, recall in Baptism that there is a *vis fluens*, a power flowing through the water during the sacrament that, with the words, justifies the recipient, making him or her a child of God and free of original and subsequent sin. What if the water during baptism were conscious? What if the water knew that it was being used as an instrument of salvation? If the water subsequent to baptism said, "It was nothing. I am just ordinary water. Nothing fantastic to see here." This would not be humility. It would be a lie. If on the other hand the water began to think that he had the power himself to regenerate souls and make them participants in divine life, he would be sadly mistaken. That foolish pride would also be a lie.

The great joy of the priesthood is precisely as instrument. A priest gets to do things—is enabled and empowered to do things—that are so much greater than him. He must remain ever aware of both his weaknesses and the Divine greatness coursing through him. He is an earthen vessel that God employs precisely to manifest that the power comes from him alone. To see this, to be conscious of this, is to be a man of prayer. Priests must, as St. Charles Borromeo stated, meditate before and after sacerdotal activities. This alone allows the man to see both the magnificence of divine action and so be humbled, while at the same time to see how he is used and so drawn to magnanimity. That tension, while not essential for the efficacious nature of the sacraments the priest administers, is necessary for his own sanctification as an active participant in the action. There is an intimacy a priest has with Christ and his passion, as one who calls him, holds him, and gives him; that is the office of a dear friend.

One being alone knows this reality: his Mother. The Blessed Mother is the perfect compliment to his passion with her perfect compassion. She knows perfectly what it is to offer him. In his final gift, Christ having accomplished our redemption, gives his Mother to John. How close she is to priests. How attentive to their growth. She does not attempt to save them from suffering. She raises them to be in his image, to offer as he offers, to sacrifice as he sacrifices. "Woman, behold your son," he says, and "Son, behold your Mother." Mother look to these my friends and love them, friends look to my Mother, your Mother, and learn to love as she loves. In beholding her, you will behold the Church and learn to love her. In beholding her, you will learn how to be a son of God, a son of Mary. Another Christ.

CONCLUSION

St. Thomas Aquinas notes that the sacraments are to divine life what basic essentials are to our natural life. We are conceived, born, grow, age, and die, and for each of these stages there are basic needs such as food, water, comfort, social interaction, and care. All these are required each in their own measure as we grow; for example, the food of a child is not that of an adult. Similarly, divine life is conceived in us, we are born into it, and it requires nourishment and at times healing. But as the natural life of our body begins to break down with age, the divine life in us has the capacity to grow ever stronger and youthful.

What stage are you in your human life? What stage are you in your divine life? Have we crested in terms of bodily growth but our supernatural life is that of an infant's? We have tended since infancy to our natural life but few are so diligent with their supernatural life. By way of conclusion, I offer the following points to assist you to engage the sacramental life that you might truly have life—divine life—and have it in abundance.

ENGAGING THE SACRAMENTS IS INCARNATIONAL

We saw in our treatment that the sacraments are the extension of Christ's work. His humanity is a visible and tangible reality, the very instrument of God. This means that our engagement of the sacraments must have all of the incarnate elements as we (like unto his human nature) must be receptive to his divine activity. Practically speaking, it means that each bodily action matters. The sacraments, as we saw, have set matter and form.

But what about our participation? Does it *matter* whether I skip Holy Mass when on vacation? Does it matter what I wear to Holy Mass? Does it matter whether I make visits to the Blessed Sacrament? Does it matter whether or not I examine my conscience and make a good confession once a month? Does it matter whether I pray daily at my bedside, at my desk, in my car, or on the plane? Does it matter if I make the sign of the cross and offer a benediction when at a meal in a restaurant? Does it matter what mental chatter I engage in concerning my parish priest or my neighbor at Mass? Does it matter if I sit, lie, stand, or kneel when I pray? Does it matter what I was doing before arriving in church or when I leave from Mass and what I do afterwards? Does it matter if I do that novena every day for nine days? Devotions? Flowers to the Virgin?

I think you see the point. It all matters. We are not angels. We are men and women. Everything we do we do in our bodies and that matter matters. Have a bridegroom tell his bride he wants no "pomp and circumstance." Let him tell her he prepared nothing for the wedding and wants nothing. It is the thought that counts. He wants no flowers, no dresses, no decoration, no champagne, no music, no dancing, no tuxedos, no nothing. What has he told her? Namely, that the event is not worthy of expenditure. It is not worthy of celebration. It is not worthy of sacrifice. It is not worthy of love.

Recently, I was in a sacristy at the shrine of one of my favorite saints. I had a Holy Mass scheduled there but had forgotten to bring my own vestments. The sacristan was not pleased. Long before she arrived there, I had lived at that shrine for a summer. As such, I knew where everything was in the sacristy and knew they were well stocked. I kindly asked for the required vesture, but she said they had nothing of the sort. I told her where it was and she looked surprised. She said she had no intention of using those things. She would have to wash them, iron them, and fold them afterward. She said she had no time for such nonsense and that she was grateful that the chaplain of the shrine was simple and didn't go in for all of that bother. I asked her a simple question. "About what else should we bother? What else, if not the supreme sacrifice of a God who offered himself as an immolation for your sins and mine? What else is worth the effort if not this? She just stared at me, stunned I think. I hope it was a seed that went to her heart.

Everything matters. Make visits to the church when no one sees you. Offer flowers to Our Lady when no one is looking. Use holy water and kneel in your room where your Father sees you, and your Father will reward you. Each movement of your body in prayer is liturgical. Offer to him your bodies as a "living sacrifice." This is sacramental living. Then bring that trained body to the sacraments and engage them in all of their incarnate reality.

ENGAGING THE SACRAMENTS REQUIRES PATIENCE

Speed. We love the instantaneous service, the internet, the movie on demand, the reply to our text or our post. We love the immediate. But sacraments by definition are "mediated," not immediate. Remember that you are attempting to engage the God to whom a thousand years are as a day. He creates over the course of ages what to him is always now. He is not in a hurry. He is the God of eternity. Thus, he can speak of his second coming as if it were tomorrow. He is the God who created seeds when we want food now. He makes us wait. With no signs of life. Waiting, hoping, trusting. He is the God of the embryo. We cannot even know the face of our own children nor their sounds for months. But he does know them. He is the God of parables who release their revelation over the course of ages by meditating monks who slowly scribble insights achieved after years of faithful vigil. He is the God who rewards the persistent, the one who knocks on the door indefatigable and undaunted by the silence on the other side.

Sacraments take time. I am not referring to the length of Holy Mass or the long wait in the confession line. Their effects are like life. I do not change my diet and engage a rigorous exercise plan and expect to see results by the end of the first day, at least not if I am living in reality. Health and strength come at the price of persistence and regularity. It is true that God can change the heart in an instant, but this is extraordinary. The ordinary means are the sacraments, which work on the principle of fidelity. Fidelity does not mean "going through the motions." This is matter and no form. He must have your heart. As the old adage goes, if the heart is not praying, in vain do the lips labor. Fidelity is the man to his wife of forty years. Fidelity is the mother to her child in sickness and pain. Fidelity means you must water the seeds every day when you see nothing. You must protect them and care for them once they are seedlings. You must pick the fruit at the proper time and wait for it. It does take time. But growth is certain. Nature does not fail in things necessary. Much less does supernature.

We are not accustomed to this. We do not grow food. We do not live by the seasons. We do not read poetry and search for meaning. We do not watch sunsets except to take a selfie. We do not attend to things for long anymore. We do not even attend to those we love for very long. Our conversations are like a game show. We are given seconds to say what we wish to say and hope it is received before the buzzer of a text comes in and we have lost the round of attention to the latest interloper. We used to call this rude. We once taught it was bad form to interrupt a conversation. No longer. We have all surrendered because we are all retreating from the world of time, patience, and meaning for the new stimuli of the instantaneous.

But this will not work with the sacraments. You cannot pray this way because God will not play this way. He requires you when you come before him. Nothing more and nothing less but all of you. To focus you on him even if just for a moment. What happens as a result of that encounter in the sacraments is like unto a real encounter with a real person. We are changed. We consider it. Something in us is better or worse for the meeting. In the case of God and his sacraments, we are no doubt better, but we may not feel it. It takes time.

It is not just moral or didactic, it is also something working inside us. It is grace. But grace is often as slow as the growth of a tree. You never notice it unless you leave for years and return. When did the tree grow? You never saw it move. Yet it was growing all the while with ring after ring of strength.

If you try to get through a sacrament by filling it up with other things, reading the bulletin (for the baby boomers), checking your phone (everyone after the baby boomers), day-dreaming or chatting, it will seem long, but your encounter will be short if at all. You must give yourself to it completely. Allow nothing else to come to the sacrament with you. Did those who heard his voice, watched his movements, brushed up against his side, count the time? Not those who had a real encounter. They had met the Lord of history in a spot of time and that moment was like unto eternity, which is not duration but fullness.

ENGAGING THE SACRAMENTS ABOVE ALL ELSE

As with the first commandment, God does not allow his sacraments to come second. If God is not primary as the ultimate end of every action, we suffer the consequences of having pointless action. If his sacraments are not the architectonic good, ordering our lives to the supernatural, then we have no supernatural life about which to speak. If I order Mass around a football game, a party the night before, a vacation, a sleep-in, anything, I cannot expect the effect to be great. The sacraments objectively do what they symbolize, but the ultimate effect in you is rather proportionate to your offering. You cannot give little and expect the infinite. "I don't get anything out of Mass" is the same as saying "I offer nothing." It is an exchange. It will be primary or it will not be powerful. I go to worship, not to be worshiped. I go to praise, not to be praised. It is not self-help. It is not the boutique in which I find that little something to make the ensemble of my character just right. It is not a piece of a pie in my over-all wellness wheel. It is the epicenter of my existence. I must order my life around the sacraments if I want my life to be ordered to Christ. Remember they are Christ's actions. Yet Christ was acting for three years and many a man, woman, and child passed by with little to no effect. Only those who *followed* him were altered.

There were many saints in history for whom the sacraments had so become their life that they could no longer consume normal food.[21] This is of course an extraordinary grace, but no doubt these miracles are meant to manifest that we are made to live on the Word that comes forth from the mouth of God. He is our food. He is our drink. He is our light. He is our life.

Look at your week. Does it revolve around the sacraments? Do we live the feasts of the Church as well as her fasts? Living liturgically sanctifies the time and our lives. It allows us to move with the rest of the Body of Christ through the mysteries of Christ's life. It imparts meaning and drama.

---

[21]   In J. R. R. Tolkein's *The Lord of the Rings*, the elven bread known as *lembas* was given to the wayfarers on their perilous journey. At one point when all other food had run out and they were left with only the precious elven bread, the hobbits found that such power came forth from this bread in proportion to one's reliance upon it. In other words, when they had nothing else, that flaky, seemingly insubstantial bread was sufficient alone to sustain them.

It inserts my mind into the mind of Christ and allows me to participate in his thoughts and capture the movements of his Sacred Heart.

Engaging the Sacraments Must Be Marian

The ever-Virgin Mary is the image and Mother of the Church. What she is, we must become. What she has done, we must do. The Church has long painted her poised in silent reflection, often upon the words of Isaiah, "a virgin shall conceive and bear a son." It is at this moment when Gabriel comes. It is when she is alone. When she is silent. When she is in communion with the word of God that the Eternal Word comes to her.

In *Fra Angelico*'s depiction in the convent of San Marco in Florence, the angel himself comes on bended knee with his arms folded across his breast in humble supplication. The Virgin remains seated with her hands folded, not across her breast in humility, but across her womb where the Word is about to enter. Sacraments are the Divine Word united to matter imparting divine life. This is the Annunciation. It does not happen fruitfully without the elements of receptivity, silence, desire, emptiness, longing, and obedience. Ask the Mother of the Incarnate Word to teach you. Ask her to speak to you about those moments before the angel came to her. Ask her about the moments after, just before she went in haste to the hill country in service. Ask her to make your heart, your body, and your mind like unto hers. May you who are her son, you who are her daughter, take after your Mother.